Ultra Cosmic Gonzology

Ultra Cosmic Gonzology

By Charles Giuliano

Berkshire Fine Arts, LLC
Adams, Massachusetts

berkshirefinearts.com

Copyright © 2016 by Charles Giuliano

Published by Berkshire Fine Arts, LLC

Book Design by Studio Two, Amanda Hill

All rights reserved. No part of this book may be reproduced or transmitted in any form or by any means, electronic or mechanical, including photocopying, recording, or by any information storage and retrieval system without the written permission of the author. For information or permissions contact Berkshire Fine Arts at P.O. Box 388, Adams MA 01220.

ISBN: 9780996171533

Library of Congress Control Number: 2016912035

For Astrid Hiemer as life partner, muse, mentor, and editor. And to those who have supported and commented on the work. In particular I am grateful to my sister Pip; a superb editor, Leanne Jewett; and constant consigliore, Robert Henriquez.

Contents

Introduction xiii
Gonzo Aesthetics: The Avant-Garde Poetics of Charles Giuliano xix

Family 1

    Blood 4
    Nugent Women 6
    Flynn Foundation 8
    Manet 10
    Harvest Moon 12
    Every Other Sunday 14
    Gravy 16
    My Bad 17
    Super Tuesday 18
    Mom Cracked the Whip 20
    Dad Cooked 22
    Century 24
    Anniversary 26

Friends 28

    That '70s Show 29
    New Histories 31
    Al the Arab 32
    B. B. 36
    Mondo Cane 38
    Crushed 40
    Ray, Jr 41
    Rob Moore 42

Vico	44
Harvard Mug	46
Bicycle Thief	50
Letter to Chris	47
Milestones	52
Jack Lyons	53
USS Bonhomme Richard	56
Alice's Restaurant	58

Gloucester 60

Good Harbor Beach	61
Annisquam	64
Nutcracker	66
Prodigal	68
Norman's Woe	69
Low Tide	72

Artists 74

Allen Ginsberg	75
Playwright Mark St. Germain	77
African Artist El Anatsui	80
Der Alte Stil	82
Charlotte Moorman and Nam June Paik	84
Lin-Manuel Miranda	87
Artist Rafael Mahdavi	90
Fresco Cycle	92
Playwright Robert Brustein	94
Raphael Soyer	97
Julia Child	100
Revenant	102
Polish Rider Jerzy Kosinski	105

Music 108

Son House	109
Free Willie	111
Muddy Waters	114
Buddy and Junior	116
Bobby Blue Bland	118
Chuck Berry	120
Storyville Pianists	122
Eubie Blake	124
Pianist Teddy Wilson	126
Pianist McCoy Tyner	129
Jazz Pianist Bill Evans	132
Herbie Hancock	136
Pianist Chick Corea	140
Jammin' the Jive	142

Count Basie 144
Woody Herman 148
Stan Kenton's Artistry in Rhythm 151
Buddy Rich 154
Dizzy 156
Mingus Ah Um 158
Old Blue Eyes 160
Stan Getz 162
Ray Charles and Stevie Wonder 164
Zoot Sims 167
Gato Barbieri's Last Tango 170
Janis Joplin's Last Gig 172
Tenor Titan Sonny Rollins 175
Madam Bricktop 178
Lady Day 180
Duh Ramones 182
Ella Fitzgerald 185
Scat Singer Annie Ross 188
Sarah Vaughan 190
Betty Bop 192
Carmen McRae 194
Pixie Voiced Cabaret Singer 196
Great American Songbook 198
Lou Reed 200
Lou Two 202
Modern Lovers 204
DJ Ron Della Chiesa 207
Amy and Tony Body and Soul 210
Peter Wolf 213
Jimi Hendrix RIP and Read 216
Marc Bolan's Pratfall 220
Cyndi Lauper 222
Black Star 224
Illinois Jacquet 226
OMG 229

Omnibus 231

First Communion 232
Econo Class 234
Pathfinder 235
Peacemaker 236
Bookends 238
Siesta to Semester 240
Saints 242
First Light 243
Troy 244
Contrarian 246

Fall 248
Bonsai 249
Boston 250
Unequivocal 251
Kicks 252
Subway Sirens 254
Old Miss 256
High Bush 258
Moby Dick 260
Sirens 262
Stoop to Conquer 264
Pill Popping 266
Tom Cruise for President 268
Stuff 269
Great Spirit 270
Classics 272
Penelope 275
Pope Francis 278
Obama Cried 280
Gonzo With the Wind 283
Mea Culpa 284
Making the Berkshires Great Again 286
Kid Talk 289
Degenerate Art 290
Paella 293

Collage 294

Spirit Boat 295
Royal Flush 297
Stonehenge 300
Boulders 302
Chateau Frontenac 304
Toledo 306
Amalfi Coast 308
Brandenburger Tor 310
Alpine Hotel 312
Hell's Angels 314
Kinky Boots 316
Talking Heads 318
Shanghai Dawn 320
Gardens of Suzhou 322
Marilyn in Paris 324
Captured in Stone 326
Watson and the Shark 328
Niagara Falls 330
Name Brand 333
Elvis in London 334

Blinding Blizzard 336
Lion King 338
Giverny Goes Pop 340
Odessa Steps 342
Vacationland..344
Caryatids 346
Ancient Oracles 348
London Calling 351
Limoncello 354

Seasons 356

Rastas in P'Town 357
Harvest Moon 358
Eclipse 360
Black Friday 361
The Reign in Spain 362
Outside the Lines 364
Turkeys 366
Low Winter Sun 368
Santa 370
Winter's Tale 373
Day After Christmas 376
33rd Annual Re-Rooters Day Ceremony 378
Valentine 380

W 382

Who 383
Who You 384
When 386
Why..388
Where 389
Where From Here 391
Never Neverland 392
Space Oddity 394
Shooting Into the Ranks 395
Requiem 397
Checkmate 399
Lazarus 401

Introduction

Poetry and its corollary, rock 'n' roll, are regarded, primarily, as art forms of the young. They convey the first flowers of youth springing sanguine from the rich soil of wonder, hope, lust, hubris, and insecurity.

With passionate expression, most often exploring aspects of love, there is a striving by young poets for understanding and insight that comes with time and life experience.

Consider that there are few chart-busting songs reflecting on decades of marriage and family.

Youth is in a rush to grow up, while the mature seek to rejuvenate and renew beauty, energy, and vitality. America does not allow its artists and celebrities to age with grace. In addition to nip and tuck, there is a megabucks cosmetics industry. Art reflects and grows out of the arc of life's primal, relentless progression.

How abnormal to come to an outburst of poetry during the midpoint of the seventh decade of my life. It was there before, tucked into sketchbooks, but never with the current intensity and confidence. The current motive is about looking back, putting into order adventures and insights. The poems chronicle landmarks of a road well traveled rather than speculation on what lies ahead.

Unlike most professions, artists never retire. In late works they explore projects and ideas shaded by legacy and inevitable ordering of insights and adventures. There is often drama and gravitas in, for example, the compositions of Beethoven or the paintings of Titian, Goya, Monet, and Degas. Often the humanistic inclinations are exacerbated by physical degeneration with creators responding to diminished hearing, sight, or movement.

Artists often have aesthetic responses to afflictions, phobias, or addictions. Loss is morphed into creative gain and shaded-charting of troubled waters.

The approach here is forged on the anvil of gonzology. The métier has been heated to a glowing red then hammered out on the unyielding anvil of insight and experience. Cooled as inspiration dims, the form is plunged back into the coals and fanned to malleable potential. Back on the blacksmith's metal block, words are beaten into shape with gonzo urgency and terseness. There is a staccato effort to strike while the iron is hot.

If the young are striving for love and relationships, in that greatest of artistic stages, what Albrecht Dürer depicted in the print *Melencolia*, there is a progression to the cosmic, metaphysical, and mystical. There is a search for the mystery of creation, the vast unknown cosmos. The beyond is probed by the five Ws: Who, What, When, Where, and Why.

It is what Gauguin, alone and diseased in the paradise of Tahiti, asked in the epic painting *D'où venons nous*, which I have contemplated so many times in the Boston Museum of Fine Arts, or standing riveted in the Sistine Chapel, gazing up over the altar at *The Last Judgment* of Michelangelo. Rising from their graves, the deceased either ascend to heaven or are dragged down into hell. The artist depicted himself as the flayed skin of the martyred St. Bartholomew. It is a harrowing image of the tormented artist, his flesh gnawed at by inner demons in the name of

God and salvation.

As Job's wife told him "Curse God and die."

Not long ago the rock star David Bowie released his final work *Lazarus* with an accompanying video. Given a career of so many phases, this final statement is among his most riveting, enduring, and perplexing.

Raised and educated—one would add shaped and damned—by nuns, what comfort is there for one who believes that God is dead and hell is other people? That sets one adrift in a search for meaning. Some seek an alternative in science as giving answers that faith and the church fail to provide. Arguably, science with its facts, evidence, research and experimentation can explain phenomena and cure disease but fails to assuage the fevered mind and ravaged soul.

We are left to our own devices, seeking a path through the dark forest. This has been manifest in art and literature from its beginning. Every civilization and culture has its creation mythology, rites of passage, and burial rituals.

Here these primal themes are deconstructed using gonzology, which is the pursuit, understanding, creation, critical analysis, and history of all things of, by, and related to the utter gonzo. As a style, approach, and means of poetic action, gonzo thrives, continues to evolve, and passes the baton to coming generations. Reports of its demise are greatly exaggerated.

The first poem of the gonzo cycle, "August," was written at the end of summer in 2014. By June 2015 the first book, *Shards of a Life*, was launched at Edith Wharton's The Mount. The second, *Total Gonzo Poems*, was previewed with a reading at the Williams College Faculty Club in November of that year. The third book, *Ultra Cosmic Gonzology*, is going into production during the spring of 2016.

These three books gather some 400-plus poems initially posted on *Berkshire Fine Arts*. Prior to publication all of the works were edited by me with further input from the first reader, Astrid Hiemer, and final reader, Leanne Jewett. Through this entire cycle there has been ongoing discussion with Robert Henriquez who has composed the critical essays and overviews for the three books. They have been superbly designed by Amanda Hill of Studio Two in Lenox.

The norm for books of poetry is a thin volume, the efforts and compilations of years, perhaps decades, and other than covers, sparsely illustrated. These books, however, have become progressively bigger and more ambitious, from 100 poems in the first to some 180 in the third. Each book has represented a finality as well as a beginning.

Now perhaps there is an end. The driving force of a range of themes has been explored. In the beginning there were obvious subjects, family, self experiences, seasons, encounters as a jazz/ rock/ blues, and arts critic. The current book adds photo-collages, cosmology, and geriatrics. Much of this terrain is no longer terra incognita.

As Henriquez commented during a time when rock stars from Bowie to Prince were falling, "They're shooting into the ranks." He has suggested to me there will be new and more challenging paths to follow.

On many levels the images in these books are equal in weight to the writing. In general, images preceded and inspired the text. That has entailed exploring and photoshopping family archives and albums. There is a body of work photographing musicians and artists in performance, as well as during encounters and interviews. As a studio artist I created an oeuvre of photo-collages. These have inspired a chapter of this book.

For every artist there is a conundrum. There is the unquenchable drive to create the work. That entails the excitement of daily visits to the studio or computer. That inevitably raises doubts about the merit of the work. My career has focused on writing criticism of the work of others.

Some years ago I was included in a group show at the Boston Center for the Arts. Confronting the critic for the *Boston Phoenix* I asked why he wrote about all of the other artists but failed to mention me. His answer was "You can be a critic or an artist but not both."

It is a complex question for which, hopefully, these books present an argument. Their value is not for me to say. Along the way peers, colleagues, and readers have been generous with support as well as advice.

Many actors tell me that they do not read their reviews. Both positive and negative comments tend to shape and distort their efforts. Some critics think of themselves as surrogate directors, editors, and producers. This is an approach that I have come to avoid.

The obligation of the artist is to be clear and true to the work. Its value and insight will be left to the audience, viewer, listener, and reader. At the end of the day, we do the best we can.

Gonzo Aesthetics: The Avant-Garde Poetics of Charles Giuliano

An Essay by
J.M. Robert Henriquez
Written for *Ultra Cosmic Gonzology*
By Charles Giuliano
2016

With his two previously published books of poetry, *Shards of a Life* and *Total Gonzo Poems* (2015)—and now with his third and latest selected poems, *Ultra Cosmic Gonzology* (2016)—Charles Giuliano has led us through an outburst of poetry recounting the wisdoms and excesses of his rich and eventful life. During this rapid accretion of poetic energy, Giuliano, a hipster septuagenarian well into the age of decreased creativity and mobility for most, has compiled, in the span of three years, a vast anthology of more than four hundred poems. These are like discrete flashes of a newly manifested type of creative energy casting a wide shine on the possibility of an avant-garde approach or style in Giuliano's poetics. Let me posit here that the ideal conditions for framing Giuliano's work in a contemporary avant-garde praxis rest in part on the peculiarities of the word "gonzo."

As a point of thorny contention, the matter of rightful ownership and meaning of the term "gonzo" still persists. For decades the word gonzo and the thoughts attributed to it seemed mired in semantic confusion. By all accounts the etymology of the word itself is not without its problems. Although now encompassing multiple meanings, the word gonzo was first uttered as an expression of defiance and victory by Giuliano—a phonetic utterance, so to speak. It appears to be at times a "signifier" in search of a determinant "signified." The etymological account of its development through the years delineates a pattern of radicalism that keeps it outside the norms of bourgeois society. Giuliano, a scion of bourgeois affluence turned progressive radical, would boastfully lay claim to the word's provenance and fate, knowing all the while that gonzo is not to be a bourgeois word. He made his case in the poem "Birth of Gonzo"—(*Total Gonzo Poems* pp. 244–245), and other published articles dating back to the 1970s. He supports his claim with due diligence by publishing three volumes of poetry, which should put any linguistic issues to rest. Now that Giuliano has introduced the word "gonzology" into the fray, is it possible for the word gonzo to earn its own "ism" suffix and be absorbed in the Western praxis of literary art? Or is gonzo the banner word to be carried at the top of Giuliano's poetic exercise and used to mark an eventual bid for an avant-garde praxis? My answer to the latter is yes, and gonzo is the de facto operative word.

Assuming, for the sake of argument, that the gonzo poems as a whole form a theoretical reasoning to advance a putatively new poetic avant-garde. Then what's needed, in this case, is an argument of convincing possibility that connects Giuliano's poetics to avant-garde practices. To begin with, the term avant-garde, which identifies trends and movements ahead of their time, is also complicated and overused. Moreover, the term avant-garde always refers to group formations—groups of artists banding together to overturn the status quo of the Establishment. The conception of an historical avant-garde is an effort to invariably assert the historical authenticity of art as a radical power for change. That said, most of the avant-garde movements that have successfully challenged the academies throughout the twentieth century—from Dadaist, Futurist, Surrealist to Beat, Lettrist, and more—have been somewhat sublated into established norms, such as "Experimental Literature," in the case of poetry.

Central to regarding gonzo poetics as a neo-avant-garde practice is in the categorical authority of the new. In a non-traditionalist contemporary society, aesthetic tradition is deductively questionable. The new gains its authority not by negating prior artistic exercises, as styles often do; it essentially negates tradition as an inescapable fact of history. To that end, the authority of the new ratifies the contemporary principle in art. Gonzo poetics by all accounts is new and invariably radical, oppositional, and non-traditional. Giuliano recognizes newness as an aesthetic category of contemporary art. One that is grounded in hostility to mainstream values and traditions characteristic of "bourgeois-capitalist society." As a new poet, Giuliano laments the reflexive negativity coming from a putatively uptight orthodoxy. By his own words he fiercely defends his position to inveigh against tradition: "Dissent is the essence of social, political, and artistic progress … Ultimately it is not the academy that prevails but the efforts of artists to subvert and destroy it … There is joy in anarchy … We must destroy in order to create anew."

Gonzo is not a movement (not yet anyway), nor is it connected to any other avant-garde groups. It is a brand-new poetic practice with its objective and methods pointing toward a bebop tempo of "asyntactic poetry." Clusters of words are strung jointly in a proprietary way to become language. Language, in turn, dictates meaning, thus keeping it all in context. Key aspects of Giuliano's poetry include the idea that asemantic-poetic sentences can actually possess meaning, and that it can also be used as poetic means to revolutionize poetry itself as a model of the gonzo revolution. Verses are made of few words, at times, just one will do the trick. Digressions are frequent, but Giuliano always returns to previous moments after amplifying them with clever anecdotes and convincing narratives. There is also an underlying erudition to Giuliano's means of expression—transitions and transmutations give way to uncovering the unfamiliar. The reader must get some grasp of the subject matter at play in the poems to get the message. All of that is part of the method and style of the avant-garde.

Giuliano's affinity for generating incomparable "beats" in free-verse lines helps him in cultivating a percussive style that works its way through more than four hundred poems. There are no rules or traditions as of yet, but there is a method in the fine gonzo madness—the conception of unusual, if not extreme scenarios—that propels the poems bopward.

In his third tome of poetry, *Ultra Cosmic Gonzology*, Giuliano once again opens his world to the reader in intimate and intriguing ways. He reveals himself as an equal opportunity thinker, a master chronicler of his own life and times and, surprisingly, as an accidental poet who got it right once again, the third time around. More importantly, he may now be considered the quintessential avant-gardist creator of gonzo poetry.

Finally, let's take heed to this paraphrase: "We must dare, and dare again, and go on daring!" (Georges Jacques Danton, Paris, Sept. 2, 1792). Readers beware, you miss the beat, you forgo the bop—traditionalists be damned!

Jean Michel Robert Henriquez is a multimedia artist and broadcast media professional who relocated from New York City to the Berkshires. His broadcasting career at the CBS Television Network spanned more than twenty years. Henriquez subsequently worked in integrated advertising (broadcast, online, and print) as a freelance media consultant and art director/producer.

Essay   xxiii

Robert Henriquez, photo by Charles Giuliano

My great grandmother Mary J. Nugent and grandmother Josephine Flynn.

The young Patrick Nugent was a gentleman farmer and scion of the Rockport clan.

Family 3

My uncle Arthur graduating from B.C. Law School with his father James Nugent.

Dad, 1940s.

James Flynn, second from left, and his elegant associates.

Blood

Patrick Nugent
Great grandfather
Dead at 50 in 1900
Blood infection
Said to be from horse
He operated
Spattering blood
On open wound
Tip of his nose
Died in slow agony
Diagnosis questionable
May have been
The Irish disease
Hemochromatosis
The organs rust
Excess of iron
Not filtered and cleansed
Killed my cousin Ellen
Shocked the family
Into getting tested
Including me
Several have the condition
Requires regular transfusions
Literally diluting
Causes arthritis-like
Symptoms
Cooks the liver
May have taken
Many of the Irish
Presumed to die young
Of demon drink

The Nugents, seated Mary and Patrick with their grandchildren, circa 1900.

Nugent Women

Irish scamp
Whiskey and women
Scion of the clan
Working the land
Beaver Dam Farm
Rockport's evocative
Dogtown Common
Patrick Nugent
Spread his seed
Passed at 50 in 1900
Left Mary with twelve
Baker's dozen
Another by his sister
Four girls
Eldest Josephine Flynn
My grandmother
God-fearing
Hard-working
Pious women
Josephine, Julia, Mary, Catherine
Posed at his funeral
Keeping the faith
While their men
Out and about
Of that
Surely
There can be
No doubt

The Nugent women; Julia (left), Mary (standing), Catherine below, and right, my grandmother Josephine.

Flynn Foundation

Sinn Féin
Founded in 1905
By Arthur Griffith
Political arm of
Irish Republican Army
Soldiers Edward and Patrick Flynn
Brits hot on their heels
Fled to Montreal
The 1920s
From there
Helped lay track
To Concord, New Hampshire
Where Edward married
Ann Cogsley
They begat five
Edward P. the eldest
Named for himself
Then Ann, Elizabeth, Helen
The youngest
James my grandfather
Londonderry, N.H., 1873–1943
Married Josephine Nugent, 1887–1949
Heard news
Former Union Generals
Butler and French
Founded Cape Ann Quarries
Later worked
Blood Lodge
Better known as
Flynn's Quarry
Cutting the granite

That built Cape Ann
Family foundation
Erected on stone
Not sand
Generations later
Progeny of rebels
Proudly stand

The future Judge Arthur Flynn as a lad.

Manet

Rockport
Taken for granite
Flynns landed in Canada
Worked quarries in
New Hampshire
Then Rockport
Building breakwater
Mighty and strong
Against howling Atlantic
Crashing giant waves
Ran ancient tavern
In Annisquam
Grandfather James
Saloons
First Gloucester
Then Boston
I'm known for
Salons

Family 11

Great grandmother Mary Nugent, center, to her left, daughter Josephine (Nugent) Flynn with her daughter Mary (Flynn) Sullivan and son James (Brother) Flynn. To the right of Mary Nugent is Dorothy Flynn the step-daughter of Josephine Flynn.

Harvest Moon

Annisquam
Living room filled
With Flynns
Mom facing me
Opposite ends
Barked a command
Charles stand up
Pull down your pants
Phobia about wrinkles
In the knees
With a shrug
Dutiful son obeyed
Standing turned
Flashed a moon
Everyone gasped
Aunt Rita convulsed
With laughter
Cousins stunned
As they recalled
Recently during
Session of swapping tales
That Irish gift of gab
One of many
Hilarious stories
Topped by Kevin's
Call to his brother Bud
On the road
Florida to East Gloucester
I just almost killed Dad
Smothered with a pillow
Knowing Judge Flynn

Who could be harsh
We laughed but
Were not surprised

The Flynn siblings left to right Brother, Mary, Mom, and Arthur.

Every Other Sunday

Martin Mugar quoted his dad
An Armenian
That WASPS don't know
How to eat
Sad but true
No funk in blue blood
Every other Sunday
In our home
Maid's day off
Dad rattled
Pots and pans
Started the sauce
Saturday night
Slowly simmering
Italian Wedding Soup
With tiny meatballs
While we went to church
Pious Catholics
Fearing hell
Dad took chances
Staying to tend
The kitchen
Chicken basted with
Oregano and lemon
Crisp tasty skin
After the soup
Tomato sauce
Italians call it gravy
Over pasta on
Thursday dinner
Maid's night out

Out on the town
Office hours
Down stairs
Jo and I fought
Over washing up
Took forever

My father, Dr. Charles Giuliano, 1950s.

Gravy

Pip says we didn't say gravy
For red sauce
In our upscale home
Recalling Sopranos
Visiting Naples
Mob sit down
Dinner in fancy restaurant
Spaghetti al nero di sepia
Con vongole
Like my lunch in Siena
Deliziosa delicacy
Paulie Walnuts turned to Christopher
Looking at the plate of
Black pasta with tiny clams
What is this he exclaimed
I can't eat this shit
The waiters in
Napolitano dialect
Unfamiliar to
Joisey hoods
Whispered with a sneer
These fools think
They're Italian
Paulie said
Take this crap away
Bring me a plate of
Meatballs with gravy

My Bad

Family gathering
Nugents of Rockport
Second cousin Susan
When we were kids
Pushed her in the fish pond
Through a window
Watched her get spanked
Boys are such bullies
Talking with her husband
Real nice guy
Asked what I do
An artist I answered
With arrogant flair
Don't make much money
Better than selling insurance
Dramatic pause
I sell insurance
He said measured and firm
And I like it

Super Tuesday

Dr. Josephine R. Flynn
Upstanding citizen
Practiced medicine
In posh Brookline
A town actually
Something of a misnomer
Given its scale and population
Bordering on Boston
Mom called
I'm running for town council
Yes and so
I responded
Well she pressed
Will you vote for me
That depends said I
What are your
Qualifications
Shocked and angered
What do you mean
I'm your mother
Well Mom
Not the best reason
That's called
Nepotism
Abruptly
Phone went dead
Sometime later
She called again
Rather briefly
No thanks to you
I've been elected

So there
Mom served two terms
Of which today
I am of course
Rightfully proud
Mom earned every vote
Just not mine

My mother, Dr. Josephine R. Flynn, 1960s.

Mom Cracked the Whip

When visiting Mom
Well into her 80s
House in Annisquam
From car
To front door
Her waiting there
Greeting of
At least five insults
Privilege and duty
Unruly son
When will you be
A little old lady
I asked plaintively
Not her style
After giving up Florida
Lonely winters
In the house
Pip came every day
After school
Just up the hill
Helper in the morning
Fixed breakfast
Pip made dinner
Got her ready for bed
Nights on the porch
Favorite TV
Never missed Masterpiece
Loved 60 Minutes
Books on tape
Keeping up
Sharp and alert

When will I see you
Imploring as we departed
That final visit
With Astrid
Lobster and a martini
Before inevitable night
Slipping into that
Other place
With soft goodbye
To each of us
Still lingers

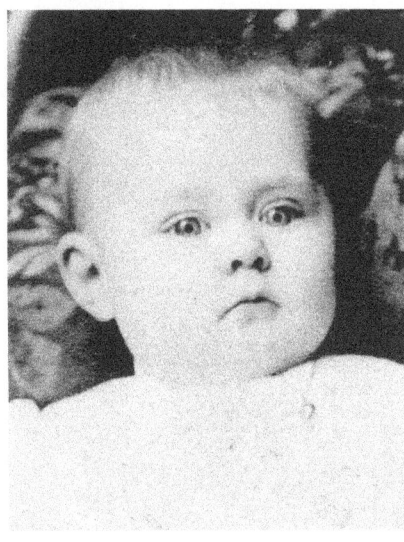

Mom as an infant.

Portrait of Mom by Marion Steele. She said, "I don't know who she is but I like her."

Dad Cooked

Dad not big on shopping
No presents under the tree
For Jo, Pip and Me
Red envelopes
Crisp with cash
1760 Beacon Street
Our office/ home
Snowed a lot in the '50s
My job to shovel
Path for the patients
Light the porch
Dug out the cars
Christmas Eve
Candles in the windows
As we strung lights
Draped tinsel
Wrapped presents
Toys for Pip
From Woolworths
At Coolidge Corner
He made eggnog
With real eggs
A splash of booze
Like we had last night
Astrid and I
Toasting the holidays
Gluten-free soy milk
Laced with dark
Meyer's rum
Dad's Sicilian caponata
Eggplant, celery, tomato, capers

Mushrooms and olives
On toasted bread
Appetizer
Family dinner
With our cousins
Pip and Ellen
Played doctor
Thoroughly examining
Young Dennis
In Mom's office
With real instruments
During meal
Uncle Jimmy said
Hey Doc this is great
What is it
Marinated octopus
The Sullivans gasped
Spit it out
Visions of
7,000 Leagues Under the Sea
No fun to dine
With the Irish
So corned beef and cabbage
After dinner
Dad at the piano
Christmas songs
We sang along

Century

Grain of sand
On the beach
Of space and time
Way of measuring
Human progress
Few cross that line
Lives spanning
A daunting hundred years
Now having reached
Three quarters
Of that challenge
Better understanding
My aging mom's
Five-year plans
At eighty told me
All down hill from here
Remained alert
Bright, engaged and feisty
Into her nineties
Retired physician
Lobster and martinis
Until the very end
Loved books on tape
Never missed
Masterpiece Theatre
Yesterday Rikki Rudd
Beloved by all
Mother of the artist Eric
Passed at 102
Such a grand dame
Of Danish heritage

Journalist and potter
Skydiving to celebrate
Turning ninety
Such an inspiration
Those magnificent ladies
Joining the cosmos
An infinity
That awaits us all

Pip and Mom in Annisquam.

Anniversary

The zinnias this summer
Just sensational
Wonders of symmetry
Complex geometry
Bursting with color
Astrid like her mother
Masterful floral arrangements
Always inventive
With weeds and wild grass
Years ago in East Boston
On Wednesdays
Before evening classes
Commute to Lowell
Always bought a bouquet
Asian flower stand
T-stop at Arlington St.
Glances from women
On the Blue Line
That knowing look
Such a nice man
Taking home flowers
Running gag
Knock on the door
Bouquet thrust through
Surprise that wasn't
Until the week I forgot
Or the anniversaries
That lapsed
Like the one this weekend
She reminded me
Making plans

I asked how many
It seems eighteen
That September 19
A Saturday like this year
In our backyard
Under the apple tree
Plus a few years of
Living in sin
When I charged rent
For a room of one's own
In our three decker
Before we got hitched
Which nixed that
Saying it with flowers
Doesn't always work
Now I buy them at
Big Y during the
Dead of winter
Bleak in the Berkshires
A bit of color
To brighten the loft
And our lives
For decades now

Cake of 70's party

That '70s Show

70 candles on the cake
Mass celebration
Hosted by Jim and Kathleen
Tent in the woods
Blown away
Old and new hipsters
Generations in the Berkshires
Gathered in Sheffield
A bridge too far
I told Jim Jacobs
AKA Shango
Who insisted we come
Sent Jessie
Sprightly kid
Salad chef
Son of Rick and Laurie
Skinny and ripe
Handlebar mustache
Nicely waxed
Round trip from Pittsfield
Begged us to stay
An hour more
At least till end of set
Astrid dancing nonstop
Last meeting of the clan
Many from the annual
Celebrations with
Benno and Stephanie
Just down the road
The venerable G
Leaning on a cane

In from Hudson
Driven to and fro
By Asako
Talk of a visit
Seeing Alan and Lynn
The brothers Jacob
Catching up
Comedies of errors
Bernie now into real estate
Dinky a rock legend
Took stars on tour
Couple from Miami
Lost at the airport
Staggered in
Late for Indian buffet
All those studs
Their rocker queens
Boogied late
Into the summer night

New Histories

Some time back
Lunch with
Long lost friend
Shared memories
Nostalgia for times
Long gone
Good laughs
But I said
Remaining friends
Means
Creating new
Histories
Without which
No reason
To meet more often than
Chance encounters
At parties
Or funerals

Al the Arab

Cardoso pulled up
Boosted short
Cool crib
Speedway Avenue
Out popped
Al the Arab
Full grown
From the head of Zeus
So called for
Levantine aspect
May not have been
Yanoff says
Probably Armenian
Or Lebanese
Ever impeccable
Fastidious in detail
No bread
Lived on air
Kindness of strangers
Hipster wizard
Master chemist
Ether to O
Wicked hash
Artist and musician
Gypsy mandalas
Conjured on his
Violin
Great pains with
His lid just so
Steamed and creased
Wisps of hair

Tucked under
Spanish boots
Kicks neatly polished
Sorcerer's apprentice
Particularly language
Exotic ergot
Astonishing patois
Rolling off the tongue
Transformed my
Bourgeois vocabulary
Subway a rattler
Endless talks
Art and music
Crafty inventions
Labored over
Device for violin
Relief of pressure
Distorting neck
Kept breaking
Repaired teeth
Epoxy and tinfoil
Back on holiday
Christmas season
Al holding court
Crystal ball
On pedestal
Surrounded by lights
Twinkling in the night
Hand laid on
Uttering oracles
Then a laugh

More like a chortle
Not so funny when
Pounders knocked
Down the door
On the lam
Down and out
Lower East Side
Neighbor and mate
Walked mean streets
Me sanguine paced
Al berating
You're race-horsing me
He the thoroughbred
Prancing prince
Led to the gate
Lost track of him
Back in Southie Projects
Off the radar
With his Mom
No marker
Pauper grave
These words
As monument
Now shade in
Gonzo heaven
Hipster's inferno

Al the Arab. Giuliano drawing, 1960s.

B. B.

Stray dog
Mostly shepherd mix
Hopped on the T
Off at Arlington
Followed the crowd
To Tea Party
Managed by Steve Nelson
Back in '68
That night blues man
B. B. King
Curled up for a snooze
After the set
Wandered into dressing room
Nuzzled the musician
Soul brothers
Steve took him home
Named him B. B.
Came to know all the haunts
Including my basement crib
Murder building
Harvard Square
Up to open the door
B. B. racing past us
Knowing his spot
Curled up in the kitchen
As true a friend as Steve himself
So content when visiting
Dog mostly human
Streetwise and insightful
Glad to hang with hipsters
Hellhounds on the run

Finally old and worn
Riddled with disease
Slow on the move
Feeling too much pain
While Steve and Jan were out
That night
Bolted through an open window
Knowing when to check out
On his own terms
Paws for memories

Mondo Cane

Remembering the
Magnificent B. B.
Reminded me of
Jim's mutt
Known from when
I bunked with him
On Fort Hill
Back when
Young and poor
Lots of brown rice
Gathered in front of
Black and white TV
There that night
When Billis
Mostly shepherd cur
Gave birth to pups
She promptly ate
Evoking Jim's rage
At his Dogus Horribillis
The contemptible
Billis for short
Compared to
Fondly remembered
B. B.
Nature balances
With bad and ugly
Better to admire
Rare beauty
Furry ode to joy

Steve Nelson and B. B., photo courtesy of Nelson.

Crushed

In a van with
Dave, Jim and John Chamberlain
To Donald Judd's studio
Fastidious craftsman
Galvanized metal cubes
Elements for sculpture
Failed inspection
Gave them to John
Drove to Canal Street
Recycling center
Used paper compactor
Put boxes in
One at a time
Chamberlain crushed them
Light hand on the switch
Shifted around
Studied from every angle
Getting it just right
Loaded them in the van
Took some skill
Awkward shapes
No longer pristine
Back in John's loft
Rejected Judds
Morphed into
Chamberlains

Ray, Jr.

Cambridge roommate
The smashing Phyllis
From Newton
Met at Saturday classes
MassArt
During high school
Student at RISD
Dated Ray, Jr.
Son of the Don
Her apartment
Broken into
Looted of stuff
Cried to boyfriend
Next day
Word on the street
Again a break-in
This time though
Everything put back
Just where it was
Nobody messes with
Girlfriend of a
Patriarca

Rob Moore

Other ends of a couch
Dinner party
After an opening
Matching Perry Ellis suits
Rob Moore's a Santa Fe brown
The color of earth
Mine lime sherbet
Bought at
Filene's Basement
We laughed about that
He was tipsy
So fine and handsome
Elegant Southern accent
Dripping with Spanish moss
You know Charles
Staring me down
When I had my first show in Boston
You described my work as
Resembling Navajo rugs
But you said
Navajos did it better
Review long forgotten
Artists know them
Chapter and verse
Rob died young
January 1, 1993 at 55
Complications of AIDS
Months later
Retrospective at Mass Art
Respected professor
Geometric abstraction

Asked to review it
Art New England
Looked long and hard
Perhaps really seeing
Writer's block
Daunted by responsibility
Went back
Got it right
Rob never saw that review

Vico

Sunday brunch in P'Town
Vico and Grace
Glorious late September
Artists, colleagues and friends
Memories of visiting
Them in Florence
Vico made soup
From stale bread
Talk of recipes
Polenta rather than pasta
From the Piedmont
Northern Italian
Different than Grace
Like me a Sicilian
Whole compared
To my half
Tale of when
Vico worked at
Sal's restaurant
Not speaking
Much of the English
Fresh off the boat
Ecco with a shrug
Late night mopping up
Two thugs barged in
The big one well known
Local bruiser
Sancho Panza sidekick
Said beat him up
Vico cringed
Looks exchanged
With hand gestures

His unique semaphore
Shrugs and gasps
Punctuating the narrative
Beat him up
Again but more insistent
Vico blurting out
Something in Italian
Then, Miracolo
Si, si with a shrug
The big guy embraced him
Italia e bella non e vero
In broken languages
Memories of Italy
They wandered off drunk
Into the night intent
On beating someone
With luck and pluck
Pinocchio survived
To tell the tale
With gusto

Vico Fabbris in Provincetown.

Harvard Mug

Me and Phil Bleeth
Titubating hipsters
Strolling the Square
Eons ago
Students selling
Fancy Harvard mugs
Ornate and expensive
Let me see one
Grabbed it and split
Thief on the run
Outrageous stunt
Street theatre
Of the absurd
Performance art
Turned around
Phil cracked up
Frozen in place
Doubled over
Held hostage
Not hip to the scam
Happened too quick
Jammed up accomplice
I walked back
Handed it over
Ruined the gag
Grabbed a beer
Still laughing
Decades later
By e-mail to
Thailand
Where he lives
On the lam

Letter to Chris

Dear Chris
Just saying hello
For no good reason
Noting recent interactions
Live and by e-mail
Past and present
Snake shedding skin
Outer personas
Detritus of human nature
Same DNA within
Bound by past
Never shaking free
Always intent to invent
Since August 2014
First book, 100 poems
Second due soon another 137
Since going to press
As of today 52 more
Actually now 53
If you count this
Not making sense
Blimey
As Jane Baker says
From Bournemouth
Or Jane Hudson
Rifkin adding comments
Robert says nothing
Astrid smiles
Larry shrugs
On to next book
For perhaps

Another hundred people
Vanity projects
Fool's errand
Satisfying nonetheless
Outrageous
In some ways
Given the drift
Perhaps not at all
Trivial compared
Whoosh
Time zooms by
Into a void
Not making sense
Who gives a damn
We totter and dodder
Looking for love
In all the wrong places
Bright October day
Nothing to be done
Best
Charles

Chris Busa. Giuliano photo.

Bicycle Thief

Merde
The first word of
Ubu roi
Alfred Jarry
Opened and closed
December 10, 1896
Alain Didot
French Adonis
Exclaimed
Emerging from
Brattle Theatre
Where we saw
Fellini film
Bike stolen
He copped another
Pedaled home
Cambridge crib
Walls decorated
Engraved invitations
Paris soirees
With frail Ravi
Crammed into my
Quirky Alfa Romeo
Drove to P'Town
Slept in the dunes
First light
Back in town
Portuguese bakery
Hot bread
Dawn on the docks
Later an heir

Money laundering
Business trip
Fell by
Lower East Side
Hand-tailored suit
With Susan
Elegant restaurant
Not the same
He morphed
An aristocrat
Loft had no phone
She knocked on the door
In tears said
Alain like Gatsby
Drowned in his pool
Exquisite corpse

Alan, now deceased, and Jim Jacobs. Giuliano photo.

Milestones

Woke up this morning
Hacking and coughing
First day of 75th year
October 25, 2015
Birthday shared with
Picasso and Jonas Salk
Francoise Gilot
Lived with both
Blew me off in a Gallic huff
When we met
Her loss so it seems
Jane is right behind me
We will commiserate
Like decades back
Wrote out checks
Thirty Years and No Sense
Burned in the fire
At Benno's
Time for new rituals
Landmarks yet to be met
Five-year plans
As Mom said
On this occasion
Marking beginning
And the end
Home stretch
Much to be done

Jack Lyons

Hollywood Insider
Nimble and quick
Strolling Broadway
Mid-eighties
Me breathless
Keeping pace
Vaulting candlesticks
Backstage at Hamilton
With Leslie Odom
Knows his
Mother-in-law
Old friends
Got us tickets
Great seats
Hottest show in town
Or Sardi's lunch
Introduced
Kathleen Chalfant
Breakfast this morning
Hashing it out
In every sense
Over easy
Corned beef with eggs
Tall tales
Like Shecky Green
From the hood
Decades later
Recalling Chicago
Your dad was a cop
The comic said
They met

On the steps
Hello and goodbye
Moving in and out
Of same apartment
Onstage in Vegas
Telling the story
What are the odds
I got a million
Jack drolled
Spry and feisty
Evoking
Milton Berle
After breakfast
Back to the left coast
Supper in balmy
Palm Springs
Land of coconuts
A desert Ratso Rizzo
With a twist
Lonesome Cowboy
Remembering beloved
Jeanette

Backstage at Hamilton with actor Leslie Odom and critic Jack Lyons. Giuliano photo.

USS Bonhomme Richard

Creators
Like sharks
Have to keep swimming
It's how we survive
Jonas a Great White
Flew in for lunch
Puddle hopper
He made from a kit
Saw him land
Calm day but turbulent
Potholes up top
At 2,000 feet he said
Astrid told me
Don't fly with him
This time
Wicked cool though
Driving to the club
Nice place to hang
Great buffet
Update of
Ever more ambitious
Projects and portfolios
Trained at Brown and RISD
Under Harry Callahan
Plans for showing
Early Chicago series
Comments about latest
Online portfolio
Three weeks on
USS Bonhomme Richard
Some 500 images

Faces among the 5,000
Sailors and Marines
Young and brave
Deployed at sea
Ready to fight and die
If need be
Defending you and me
Stunning images
Take no side
On divisive politics
Roiled by terrorism
Opposites attract
Lion and lamb
Eden in Williamstown

Jonas Dovydenas flew in for lunch. Giuliano photo.

Alice's Restaurant

Fiftieth anniversary
Can you believe it
Alice's Restaurant
Concert at the Colonial
PBS broadcast
I spoke to Arlo
Shango said
Alice's Breast Flaunt
Scandalous article
Trashed our friends
Tabloid journalism
You wrote it
Both laughing
No I didn't
Protesting yet again
False accusations
Among many
Through the years
Come on Big
You know you did
More laughter
Now out of hand
Yet again
At my expense
Added to
Bad stuff on me
Much of it true
Just ask anyone
Beast of the Berkshires
But not this one
Never flaunted

Alice's breast
Not even tempted
Oh come on admit it
No way
Cop to it Big
It's just a part
Of your legend
Ok then
I didn't do it but
Yes to everything
Else

Fisherman's Memorial.

Good Harbor Beach

Most who settled
Cape Ann
Toiled the sea
Fishermen of Gloucester
Clusters of homes
Along the shore
Interior vast and empty
Dogtown Common
Abandoned in 17th century
Cellar holes and stone walls
All that remain
The Nugents
Patrick and Mary
Immigrants from Ireland
Married in 1875
Rented Beaver Dam Farm
In Rockport
From the Babsons
Until the widowed matriarch
Died in the 1920s
Of nine children
That survived their twelve
Most left farming
Migrated to other
Cities and trades
George bought property
Across the road
Now Nugent Stretch
Raised pigs and cows
A great wedge of land
Including all of

Good Harbor Beach
View of Twin Lights
Ever more popular
With summer bathers
For decades city
Maintained it then
Sued to own
Dragged on for years
Finally as reported
April 10, 1939
Charlie Nugent
Settled for $35,000
Son of a beach
Now cost fifteen bucks
Just to park
If you can find a space
All that's left
Is the Nugent name
And just a tad of
Gloucester fame

Astrid photographing.

Annisquam

Cul de sac
Village
From Algonquin
Quiet Water
Not just name
Stolen long ago
Summers
Where I grew up
Last night
Prodigal son
Returned to read
Packed Village Library
Family and friends
Perfect strangers
Introduced by Pip
Tales of wild youth
Growing up absurd
Breaking the rules
And a few hearts
Stories brought smiles
Familiar names
Local settings
The tack not taken
Sailing away from the fleet
Not settling for second
All or nothing
Washing dishes
At the club
Tossing every other one
Shards seen at low tide
Later cousins gathered

In a circle telling tales
Rare gathering of clan
Soaring night
Rare remembrance
Rampant youth
Stooped with age
Poet Geoffrey said
Slow down next time
You had them
Not taking advice
Why start now

Downtown Gloucester.

Nutcracker

No swans by
Annisquam River
Less like
Nutcracker the ballet than
Scrotum scrunching
Ballbuster
Last swim
Brisk August plunge
Summer visit
Steps from the Inn
To rocky
Cambridge Beach
Picking my way
Cautiously
Tender bare feet
Looking for sand
Avoiding sharp rocks
Wading in
Shivering mightily
Convulsed with cold
Warmest water of summer
The locals say
Brisk Atlantic
No mercy for bathers
Up to my waist
Johnson shriveled like
Ipswich fried clams
Wrists plunged in
Cools the blood
Adjustment for

Final plunge
Shock and awe
Merged with nature
Back where we emerged
Fish flipped onto land
Evolving to breathe
Emerged refreshed
Packed for ride home
Now harvest time

Prodigal

Back where it started
Summers decades ago
Growing up rich
And absurd
In posh
Annisquam
Either you sail
Or play tennis
Girls with names like
Heather and Muffy
Caste system
Passed along for
Generations
Where summer fashions
Never change
World rarely
Makes its way
From 127
That U-turn by the church
Into cul de sac
Where time and tide
Stand still
No beach access
For strangers
Armageddon
Passes by
Unseen

Norman's Woe

On the tow
Marblehead Race Week
Passed famous
Norman's Woe
Behind it
Hammond Castle
With friends
Visited for first time
And Beauport
The Sleeper Fantasy
Posh Eastern Point
Sites never seen
Growing up here
Busy swimming and sailing
No time for landmarks
Interesting mansions of
The bachelor Sleeper
America's first
Interior decorator
His home a showcase
For fashionable designs
A sickly child
Homeschooled
Lived with his mother
Until she died
Across Gloucester Harbor
In rural Magnolia
Hammond an inventor
Married to much surprise
A portrait painter
Lover of the occult

Often stayed in the city
While he entertained
In Gothic castle
Where Dracula
Cavorted at night
Folly built around
Grand pipe organ
In great hall
Which Larry played
During parties
Guests bathed nude
Like life-sized
Svelte bronze statue
Next to the pool
Near small dining room
Medieval feasting
During raucous holidays
Hammond and Sleeper
Fast friends
Enjoyed playing with
Organs
Of all kinds
Much it would seem
To the woe
Of briny Norman
Its siren's song
Luring the
Schooner Hesperus
To watery doom

Gloucester 71

Norman's Woe.

Cambridge Beach, Annisquam, a short walk from the inn.

Low Tide

Last morning
Brynmere Inn
Coffee and muffins
Reading papers
From spacious kitchen
View of low tide
Unobstructed
Building blocking view
Knocked down this week
To be rebuilt
Terrain still
Much as it was
When I summered here
Decades ago
Now an annual visitor
Recovering memories
Driving around Cape Ann
Hasn't changed
In centuries
Other than more traffic
Gawkers
Cluttering weekends
Still feeling private
Privileged
Sense of noblesse
Dinner at the Yacht Club
Hosted by Pip
Short walk away
Where getting a room
At the Inn
More challenging than
Admission to Harvard

The old Yankee Inn, and from the porch, a house knocked down, briefly enhanced the view.

Allen Ginsberg. Giuliano photo.

Allen Ginsberg

I saw the best minds of my generation destroyed by madness, starving hysterical naked

In Howl he said
Lunch in Harvard Square
With iconic poet
Ginsberg about to visit
Great Barrier Reef
Wearing two watches
One for each wrist
Keeping track
Both Cambridge
And over there
In two places
Always one step ahead
In town for an exhibition
I bought his Neal Cassady
In front of movie marquee
The Wild Ones
Early Brando film
Dean Moriarty in
On the Road
Richly inscribed print
Photographing his friends
Immortals he said
While still living
Beat Generation
Inspired us all
Rebel hipsters
Talk of Jack, Corso, Peter, Burroughs
Charles Olson from Gloucester

Best minds gone mad
Post war America
Eisenhower years
Growing up absurd
In suburbia
Loving James Dean and Elvis
Organized a project
Celebrating
Kerouac Festival in Lowell
Planned to borrow his work
Tibor de Nagy Gallery
And Polaroid portraits
By Elsa Dorfman
Whose studio we visited
Walking from Harvard Square
He died suddenly
Just before the exhibition
Such sweet shows
Boston and Lowell
With curator Linda Poras
Loans cancelled
Suddenly too valuable
So Elsa said
Hung my Cassady
That was it
For Allen
Consummate rebel
Who changed everything

Playwright Mark St. Germain

Breakfast at Dottie's
Downtown Pittsfield
Close to theatre
Named for him
Barrington Stage Company
Premiered many plays
From its inception
Mark St. Germain
First meeting
After opening of
Freud's Last Session
Toured the world
Great dialogue
Since then ongoing
Like today at
5 AM by email
Restless night
Comparing notes
Lives in the arts
Focusing on the work
Unique relationship
Playwright and critic
Wolf and sheep
One would think
Actually so much more
Discussing the craft
Mutual vulnerability
What it takes
Getting a play on stage
The many drafts
He let me read

Scott and Hem
Opened at Shepherdstown
Then Barrington
Changes in between
Discussing differences
Taking shape
From script to stage
Absorbing process
Evolving over time
Becoming Dr. Ruth
Best of Enemies
Dancing Lessons
The play's the thing
Make or break
Premieres
What makes them fly
The humanity involved
Its wear and tear
Started so long ago
Writing for
The Cosby Show
Never discuss that
Just about
Everything else
Mentor and friend
State of the art

Mark St. Germain. Giuliano photo.

African Artist El Anatsui

Like Joseph's
Coat of many colors
So too with
Biblical
El Anatsui
Works to be worshiped
Votive offerings
Evoking spirits
Metallic tapestries
Bits of detritus
Flattened into tesserae
Like mosaics
Recycled from
Bottles and cans
Fashioned with copper wire
Intensive labor
Studio of assistants
Taking shapes
Flowing over walls
Defining panoramas
Shimmering colors
Determined by curators
Global galleries
Museums of the world
Born in Ghana 1944
Lives in Nigeria
Late bloomer
To fame and fortune
Gallerist Jack Shainman
Grew up in Williamstown
Brought him to the Clark

Where we interacted
Speaking art's
Universal language
With African master

El Anatsui. Giuliano photo.

Der Alte Stil

Juvenalia of young artists
Fresh, bright romantic
Exploring love
Celebrating the sensual
Romeo and Juliet
Perhaps tragic
Not richly profound
Most rock 'n' roll
Whipping crowds
Into orgiastic frenzies
Sanguine youth
Raging hormones
Early Titian
Painter of color and light
Singing deep blues
Saturated reds
Early Rembrandt portraits
Proud, rich, successful
Living well in Jewish quarter
Depicting Saskia and Titus
Familial and jubilant
Young Michelangelo
Tall and magnificent
David facing Goliath
Slim youth armed
With slingshot
Slaying the brute giant
Or coy and swishy
In the Donatello
Nude with an absurd
Easter bonnet

Artists become
Old and darker
Light glazed over
Yellowed by cataracts
Lens grown opaque
Bashed and buffeted
Perhaps even morose
Der Atle Stil
Heart-wrenching
Late Rembrandt portraits
Somber and broke
Sued for Saskia's estate
Mourning son Titus
Poignant and powerful
Michelangelo's early Vatican Pieta
So refined and exquisite
Beautiful young Mary
Embracing crucified son
Compared to late
Tormented fragmented
Gut-wrenching
Rondanini Pieta
Beethoven was deaf
His majestic Ninth
How late works
Stoop to conquer
With subdued rage
Defiant old age

Charlotte Moorman and Nam June Paik

Julliard graduate
Nude cellist
Charlotte Moorman
Performed Cage
For Master's thesis
To faculty only
Unique protocol
Denied access to
Fellow students
Fear of corrupting them
Avant-garde virus
Friends with Astrid
CAVS at MIT
Also collaborator
Nam June Paik
Charlotte played him
Like a fiddle
Twitching between her legs
Bare to the waist
Spastic blinking
Smashing glass
Slapping him
With her bow
Seemed odd and comical
At the time
Iconic memories
Nobody laughing now
Multi-media performance
Masters of our time
Watching her fitted
For his TV Bra

Out there take on
Boobs Tube

Charlotte Moorman wearing Paik's TV Bra. Giuliano photo.

Nam June Paik. Giuliano photo.

Lin-Manuel Miranda

Between matinee and evening
Mob outside
Frenzy for
Hamilton
Get this
A musical about
The Founding Fathers
Toughest ticket
On Broadway
American history
Can you dig it
Ron Chernow's biography
From page to stage
Bastard mulatto
From a tiny island
Who shaped a nation
Epic battles not just
With the British
But Jefferson
Slave owner from Virginia
As were most presidents
Until Lincoln
Shot down at dawn
Across the river
Weehawken, New Jersey
July 11, 1804
Killed by Aaron Burr
Schemer and intriguer
By default
Jefferson's Vice President
Brilliant hip hop musical

Genius of Lin-Manuel Miranda
Bringing street music
American vernacular
Outsider art
Into mainstream
Changing the landscape
Reenergized
Flowers blooming
Reaching up
From a rich compost
That fertile under-culture
Yet again spawning
Unique expressions
Music and dance
Making us think
About dude on
Ten-dollar bills
Right now
How ironic
It takes a lot of
Hamiltons to see
Hottest show on
Broadway

Lin-Manuel Miranda. Giuliano photo.

Artist Rafael Mahdavi

Living with art
Giant dog in bedroom
Scratched and scored
Braille painting
Multinational artist
Colleague and friend
Rafael Mahdavi
Marais studio
Planning exhibition
Unstretched canvases
Laid out on floor
Selecting works
Rolled in a tube
Carry on to Boston
We built stretchers
Two exhibitions
Large paintings
Suffolk University
Works on paper
The French Library
Ambitious project
International art
On tiny budget
Sight Unseen
Shipped back in tube
As tablecloths
FedEx with
Minimal insurance
Avoiding absurd customs
How things are done
Changes since then

Metal sculptures
Created on his farm
Rural France
Now retired
From Parsons
More time to work

Rafael Mahdavi in his Paris studio. Giuliano photo.

Fresco Cycle

From beginnings
Generally tight and tentative
Probing for form
Compact compositions
Progressing through time
Skills honed
Ever more ambitious
The Parthenon sculptures
Metopes morphing
From archaic to classical
Fresco cycles
Loosen up
Release energy
Explore new dimensions
Giotto's Arena Chapel
In gothic Padua
Groups shuffled through
Grasping images
Studied intently
Or the Sistine Chapel
Nora the guide
Got us in when it opened
Beat the crowds
That time alone
Gazing up
Seeing the changes
A student in tears
Embraced me
Then over the altar
Years later
That view of the

Apocalypse
The artist skinned alive
As martyred
Saint Bartholomew
What happened
During the years between
Incremental changes
Coming from the work
Self as best teacher
Digging ever deeper
Letting go of
Inhibition and restraint
As body and soul
Erode and rot
Like Michelangelo
The artist as corpse
Rendered through
Plaster and paint
Twisted and tormented
Where next to go
At what cost
Flayed alive
Above the altar
Of life from which
No escape but art
Which survives
Telling its tale to tourists
The few who probe
The lower depths of
Passion and despair

Playwright Robert Brustein

Reviewing
Former A.R.T.
Artistic director
New Republic critic
Playing both sides
The now 88
Robert Brustein
Arts Fuse editor
Bill Marx
Reviewed his new play
Exposed
After Tartuffe
Riff on Moliere
A geriatric sitcom
Mildly amusing entertainment
There are issues
The contentious
Brustein always
In the thick of it
Polemics
Friends and enemies
Epic battles with
August Wilson
Among others
Produced avant-garde
Plays for A.R.T.
We were seasoned
Subscribers
Opening night series
He introduced
Often more enticing

Than the actual plays
Some were brilliant
Risk-taking
Absolutely stunning
King Stag
Pirandello
Phaedra
Most just so-so
Each season
Without fail
An utter dog
Insult to audiences
We lost it over
Peter Pan and Wendy
A ridiculous
Holiday show
For kids of all ages
Don't be fooled again
Bowwow
That was it
We quit
But Brustein
Still going
Marx
My words

Robert Brustein. Giuliano photo.

Raphael Soyer

Born in Russia
The Brothers Soyer
Raphael, Moses and Isaac
Social Realists
Artists of the WPA
So they say
Gentle genre
Workers at play
Little men
Best of their day
Evocative paintings
Cornered in an alley
Narrow streets of
Provincetown
Before he died in '87
Photographed Raphael
Hot summer day
By the sea
In suit and cap
Like it was winter
All buttoned up
Frozen in place
Perhaps intimidated
Big guy with camera
Shot for posterity
Gazing at me
Intently
Haunting expression
Survivor of pogroms
Covered his show
BU Art Gallery

Curator Pat Hills
Warned me sternly
Don't call him
Diminutive

Raphael Soyer in Provincetown. Giuliano photo.

Julia Child

PBS 1960s
Julia Child
Giant of the kitchen
Taught America
If not to cook
At least to appreciate
French cuisine
Often with homey
Pratfalls ended
Shows with
A meal on the table
A glass of wine
That high-pitched
Bon appétit
Launched my passion
For chef shows
Dining we
Cannot afford
Flavors and savors
Above our pay grade
Complexities
Of Michelin stars
Fun to discuss
With Robert
Who dined in many
Top restaurants
Days of wine and roses
Or Fast Eddy
Who keeps journals
Of great dinners
And cocktails

Domestic and international
Julia shopped
Around the corner
Jack Savenor
Personal butcher
My landlord
Who knew her meat
Julia was at least six feet
As big as me
Stood tall among
Cambridge celebrities

Julia Childs taught Americans how to cook French cuisine. Giuliano photo.

Revenant

No-name man
Anonymous
Mr. just He
Brando
In Last Tango
Raped
Maria Schneider
Ms. She
Actually Paul
And Jeanne
Butt fucked her
With butter
Lust and grief
Seeking relief
That bare apartment
Surrogate
For everything
All love
Despair and hate
Both violated
By Bertolucci
They were never
The same
She vanished
The director
Devoured Brando's
Heart and soul
Never given back
Life wasted
For a film
After that

Sanity vanished
The Horror
All he had left
Like Leo
In Revenant
Slashed and mangled
Not just
Ravaging bear
Protecting her cubs
Yet another
Pretty-boy wop
From boy
Now to man
Dragged crawling
Through muck and mud
Worked over brilliantly
By Iñárritu extracting
Performance
Of a lifetime
Ultimate sacrifice
That stunning land
Ah wilderness
From which
No traveler returns
Nevermore sane
After survival
Naked in
Belly of the horse
Emerging barely
All bloodied
Another epic

Truly Homeric
Astonishing score
Ryuichi Sakamoto
Pulsing through us
Joining the pantheon
Apocalypse Now
The Deer Hunter
What's left of
DiCaprio
Now among immortals
Great art for all time
Whom the gods loved
Once sanguine
Radiant youth
Now withered
By age
Drenched with wisdom

Polish Rider Jerzy Kosinski

Renowned works of art
Not always what
They appear to be
Dumpster diving
Deep in the archive
Where pearls lay
In buried oysters
Under the muck
Of time and neglect
Three slides resurfaced
Random shots
Brief encounter
Mid-Manhattan
Jerzy Kosinski
Dressed for success
Chatting with female
Seductive expression
Height of fame
Celebrated but
Controversial books
Like Polish Rider
In the Frick
Alleged Rembrandt
Something not right
About the horse
We concluded
In a graduate seminar
Later downgraded to
School of
So too with his books
Painted Bird or

Being There
Peter Sellers brilliantly
Chance the Gardner
May have been
Cribbed from
Lesser-known authors
It was alleged
Ill and oppressed
A suicide
Not surprising in the
Literary world
Xana Kaysen
Girl Interrupted
Reviewing his book
Decades ago
Told me that she
Spat on every page
Stumbling on
Such venom
While unearthing
Dark grainy images
Photoshopped back
To ersatz life
Fading clips
From scrapbooks
Of discredited
Faustian creators
Paying the price
Posthumous cost
Fugitive celebrity
Embalmed by
My camera

Jerzy Kosinski on the streets of New York. Giuliano photo.

Bop master Dizzy Gillespie. Giuliano photo.

Son House

Down in the Delta
Near Clarksville
Sharecroppers
Back porch pickers
Deep in Mississippi
Goddamn
Strange fruit
Church-going man
Mid-twenties
Son House
Turned to
Devil's music
Like Charlie Patton
Preachin' the blues
Twangy open chords
Slide style
National Steel Guitar
Metallic shimmer
Slurred vocals
Hellhound
Nipping his heels
Some recordings
Now and then
Early on
Nothing doing
Hung it up
Retired to Rochester
Porter and chef
Scratchin' it out
Revived in Sixties
Al Wilson taught

Him to play again
Picking up
Where he left off
World tours
Small clubs
New sides
Caught him in '69
Newport Folk Festival
Only time
Playing solo
Dazed and confused
Juked up juiced
Wigged out
Poignant and sad
Alone out there
Sinking fast
Muddy eased on
Side by side
Picked up the tune
Chimed in
Back on path
Gentle end
Led him off
Big wave to
Cheering crowd
Loving him
For what was
Stairway to heaven
Hell and back

Free Willie

B.B. King
Named his guitar Lucille
For Willie Nelson
Trigger after the horse
Of Roy Rogers
Bashed and battered
Its face hacked
Hole where
Pickin' over the years
Slashed through
Names scratched in
Weathered face
Chiseled like
Mt. Rushmore
As iconic as
Them presidents
Just as patriotic
In wacko way
Signature braids
Now gray
Same strap
Red, white and blues
Around his neck
Signature bandana
Nothing really changes
Wavering craggy voice
Indigenous Stradivarius
Crooning Outlaw Country
Lyrics sting whiplashing
Rough life
Paying his dues

Takes no prisoners
On the road again
Again and again
Whiskey River
Flowing on
Reefer madness
Up in smoke
Fine and mellow
Now 83
Survived IRS
Owed millions
Still out there

Willie Nelson. Giuliano photo.

Willie Nelson. Giuliano photo.

Muddy Waters

Field recording
Alan Lomax
Roaming the South
Bluesmen
Library of Congress
Muddy Waters
Acoustic for
Down on Stovall's Plantation
North to Chicago
Went electric
Chess Records
Rocked London
2120 S. Michigan Avenue
Stones homage
Played Boston
Birthday gig
Peter Wolf
Local bands
Helped blow out
The candles
Electric Mud
London Sessions
Backed by his
Progeny
Crossover mainstream
Never quite the same
Pure and simple
That mojo working
Down-home licks
Straight no chaser
Mississippi mud

White boys who
Play slick guitar
Don't chop
No cotton

Muddy Waters. Giuliano photo.

Buddy and Junior

Blew in from Chicago
Destination Beverly
Week at Sandy's
Hunkered down
Buddy Guy and Junior Wells
Wailing the blues
Slow start
Beginning of the week
Glum downer
Small house
Lacked inspiration
Just another gig
Junior getting testy
Knocking back shots
Cooking Saturday night
Club jammed
Full tilt boogie
Reefer in the alley
Buzz in the blue room
Junior asking for a taste
Mojo working
Soul singer
Mississippi saxophone
Buddy laying down licks
Roadhouse rumpus
Late that night
After hours
Nightcaps
Paid in cash
Packed up
Headed back to

Windy city
On the blow
Black and blues

Buddy Guy. Giuliano photo.

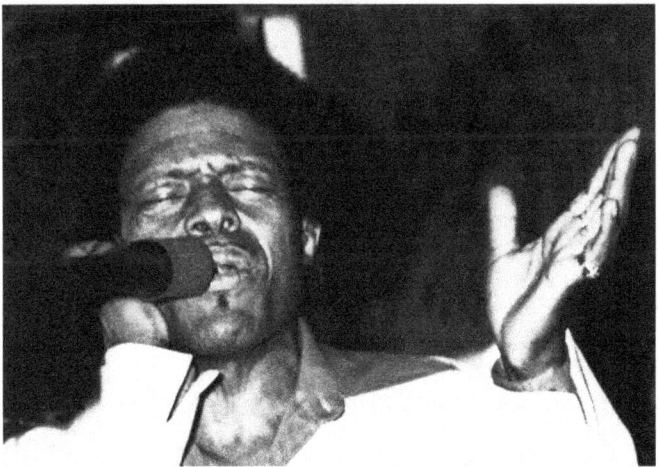

Junior Wells. Giuliano photo.

Bobby Blue Bland

Horns kicked in
Laying down a
Massive groove
Memphis blues
Smooth baritone
Clean and fresh
Bobby Blue Bland
Licking his chops
Getting the taste
Flavors of hits
I Pity the Fool
That's the Way Love Is
Soul brothers
With B.B. King
Ironic perhaps
Solid Blue
Right on
Down and dirty
Straight and true
Through and through
Bland though
What's in a name
No man
Ain't never
Preacher man
Aretha's dad
Where he got
That squall
As he called it
What took him
To the Hall

Bobby Blue Bland licks his chops. Giuliano photo.

Chuck Berry

In and out of slammer
Various beefs
Three years as a teen
Armed robbery
Later Mann Act
Jailbait
Crossed the line
With groupies
Now pushing 90
Chuck Berry
Iconic rock standards
Chicago's famous
Chess Records
Maybelline
Solid gold in '55
Teen Idol
American Bandstand
Doing the Duck Walk
Way before Michael
Same thing
In reverse
Tons of hits
Johnny B. Goode
Every garage band
Knew his licks
Hired them
On the road
Demanded cash
Upfront
Counted the money
Before going on

Performances
More like rehearsals
Now and then
Special occasions
All-star backing
Everyone jamming
On to the next gig
Greyhound bus
Just the man
And his guitar
Busted again
For tax evasion
Cash and carry
Bad luck
Can't cheat the man
Roll Over Beethoven
Tell Tchaikovsky
To fuck off

Chuck Berry. Giuliano photo.

Storyville Pianists

New Orleans
Delta Lady
Confluence of cultures
French, Spanish, Indian, Black, Creole
Red-light district
Storyville
Where jazz was born
Cathouse pianists
Professors
Rambled tunes
Jelly Roll Morton
First to stir the pot
Gumbo from classical
To ragtime
Down and dirty
Filthy and foul
Skin deep
Yet elegant
The Pearls
One such gem
Passed along
Fats Domino
Found his thrill
On Blueberry Hill
From R&B to
Rock 'n' Roll
Direct line to
Professor Longhair
Gris-Gris
Dr. John tickling
Ebony and ivory

Iko iko, iko iko unday
Jockomo feeno ah na nay
Jockomo feena nay
Right Place Wrong Time
Produced by hit-master
Allen Toussaint
Rocking French Quarter
Where every day
Dawn to dusk
Is Mardi Gras

Dr. John. Giuliano photo.

Professor Longhair. Giuliano photo.

Allen Touissant. Giuliano photo.

Eubie Blake

Well into his 90s
Eubie Blake
Put on a
Hell of a show
Rattling the ivories
Ragtime style
With Noble Sissle
First all black
Broadway hit
1921's
Shuffle Along
Revived on Broadway
Audra McDonald
Tunes like
Charleston Rag
I'm Just Wild About Harry
Basis for
Eubie!
Boffo '78 smash
Totally amazing
So full of jive
Jukin' and jumpin'
That wiggy
Dance macabre
Cakewalking
Edge of the
Abyss

Eubie Blake's *Shuffle Along* has been revised on Broadway. Giuliano photo

Pianist Teddy Wilson

Elegantly understated
Melodic lines
Pianist Teddy Wilson
With vibes of Lionel Hampton
Charlie Christian on guitar
Integrated Benny Goodman's band
Intermission trio joining
Benny and drummer Gene Krupa
Quartets with Hamp
Top of the heap
Depression years
Benny was
King of Swing
Not nice
To his sidemen
That crown
Went to his head
Teddy talked about him
With acerbic patois
Rough side to
Smooth manner
After famous
1938 Carnegie Hall concert
Legendary performance
Krupa wailing
Driving the band
Sing Sing Sing
Lester leaping in
First for jazz
Guest artists
All stars from

Duke and Count
End of an era
Band broke up
Gene, Hamp, Teddy, Harry
Fronted their own bands
War ended that
Teddy made records
Chart busters
Memorable sessions
Backing Billie Holiday
Her singular accompanist
That was long ago
Well before
We caught his gigs
In residence
Months at a time
Switching off with
Dave McKenna
Copley Plaza Hotel
Hanging with Ron
Who knew them well
There was melancholy
Giant playing
Cocktail piano
Standards for squares
Getting juiced
On the make
Too much of an edge
Daunting gap
Black in white America
Even though Teddy

Overcame barriers
They destroyed
Soul mate
Lady Day
Expressed in
Poignant music
They shared
God Bless the Child

Teddy Wilson helped to integrate the Benny Goodman Orchestra. Giuliano photo.

Pianist McCoy Tyner

Just once
With Speedway gang
Ball-busting hipsters
Fell by the
Jazz Workshop
To catch Coltrane
No cover charge
Hung by the bar
The Classic Quartet
McCoy Tyner piano
Elvin Jones drums
Jimmy Garrison bass
Amazingly for then
Set one long improv
No riffs on tunes
Familiar chords from
Standards like bop
Strung out screed
Sheets of sound
Trane overblowing tenor
Emotional reach
Stretching upper register
Embracing dissonance
The band split leaving
Garrison alone to solo
Sweating profusely
Lasted forever
They returned and
Took it out
Years later
Hanging with Tyner

At Lulu White's
Asked about Trane
They grew up in Philly
Bud Powell
Friend and neighbor
Languid style
Legato touch
Melancholy melodies
An early influence
After Miles
Gave Coltrane freedom
To stretch out
Creating new approach
Trane went on his own
Tyner recruited
Not accompanying
True ensemble playing
Pushing and inspiring
Powerful left hand
Percussive attack
Staccato right
Cluster fuck
Solid wall behind sax
Trane's extended ventures
Flights of fancy
Building on Bird
Beauty and rage
Then second drummer
Rashied Ali
More noise than music
Tyner and Jones quit

Trane dead
Just two years after
We dug him in '65
Cancer but more
Couple of years ago
Heard McCoy at
The Mahaiwe
Concert not club
Too sedate
Not the same
Lacked funk
Time has a way of
Fucking with you
Ears heart and mind
The early stuff
Hangs in
Such incredible
Head music
Where the sun
Don't shine

McCoy Tyner played with John Coltrane. Giuliano photo.

Jazz Pianist Bill Evans

From hard bop
Cluster chords
Collaborating with
Composer and theorist
George Russell
Cubana Be and Cubana Bop
Dizzy Gillespie's big band
Evolved into modal forms
Sustaining single chords
Weaving over and under
Handing off to bass
Sharing more melody
Than keeping time
Extended improvisations
Paul Chambers with Trane
Bill Evans pushing Miles
The resultant masterpiece
Kind of Blue
No rehearsals
The music evolved
In the studio
Miles gave Evans
Two chords
G minor and A augmented
That became
Blue in Green
For which
Davis took full credit
Miles looked for
Something new
Fusion and rock

Went on to
Bitches Brew
Evans avoided change
Rooted more in classical
Impressionists
Ravel and Debussy
Studied Bach
Rift with black critics
Too European
Not true jazz
No blues and roots
Classical there
From the beginning
Scott Joplin's opera
Treemonisha
Jelly Roll Morton's
Adaptations
Tiger Rag
Even the brilliant Bix
Only piano solo
In a Mist
Evoking Ravel
Later Duke's suites
Black Brown and Beige
Ultra cool MJQ
Third Stream
Conservatory jazz
Evans written out
Of black history
By Wynton Marsalis
Via Ken Burns

No room in the inn
For Bill Evans
Perhaps greatest
Pianist of his generation
Influenced
Herbie, Chick and Keith
To mention a few
That great Evans trio
Paul Motian drums
Bass player Scott LaFaro
Dead at 25
Freaked Evans
Strung out
Hands swollen
Painful to play
When we talked
Wrinkles in the legato
Labored melodies
Waltz for Debbie
Not as lilting
As it might have been
At just 51 in 1980
Died of everything
May not have been
Blues enough
For purists
Tempered by Bach
True jazz is
Color blind
It eats away
At your soul

Music 135

Bill Evans recorded *Kind of Blue* with Miles Davis. Giuliano photos.

Herbie Hancock

Looking for a new groove
Miles pushed Herbie
Made him play electric
Initially resisted
Even resented
Eventually embraced change
Transitioning fluidly
Exploring genres
Straight-up jazz
Too out there
Commercials to funk
Sound track for
Antonioni's Blow Up
Lyrical early albums
Empyrean Isles
Maiden Voyage
Standards like
Watermelon Man
Mega-hit Headhunters
Duets with Chick
In for a week
Jazz Workshop
Walked up the street
Half Shell
On my tab
Herbie ordered
Two dozen oysters
We talked about Miles
Orchestral accompaniment
Quartal harmony
Innovative chords

Second Great Quintet
1963–68
Recruited by
Boston's teenage drummer
Tony Williams
Miles liked
Emerging artists
Took them to school
Fleshed them out
Herbie thrived
Ron Carter on bass
Horns shifted
George Coleman then
Boston's Sam Rivers
Too strung out
For the road
Couldn't leave
The Man
Great player
Times I saw him
Wasted talent
Settled on
Wayne Shorter
Later formed
Weather Report
Miles fired Herbie
Flimsy pretext
Replaced by Chick
Still recorded
Now and then
That classic quintet

Reformed as
V. S. O. P.
Freddie Hubbard
On horn
Herbie still out there
Zig and zag
More changes
Than a chameleon
Struts around
Keyboard
Strapped on
Like a guitar
Moving on out
From what
Miles started

Herbie Hancock played with Miles Davis. Giuliano photo.

Chick Corea continues to experiment. Giuliano photo.

Pianist Chick Corea

Local kid
Chick Corea
From Chelsea
Miles at Harvard Stadium
Summer of 1970
Gone fusion
After Bitches Brew
Later that week
Gig at funky
Lennie's on the Turnpike
Route One roadhouse
Same group
Young Michael Henderson
Ostinato bass
Jack DeJohnette drums
Gary Bartz horns
John McLaughlin guitar
Sitting in
Later Mahavishnu Orchestra
Left and right
Fender electrics
Keith Jarrett and
Chick Corea
After the set
Hanging with Miles
He asked me
Who to get rid of
Keith or Chick
Can't keep them both
He stuck with Keith
That amazed me

Particularly as
Years passed
Corea so productive
Different phases and forms
Return to Forever
The richly flavored
My Spanish Heart
Duets with
Herbie Hancock
And other masters
Festival dates
Often paired with
Gary Burton
Always fresh
Inventive and new
Uniquely stinging sound
Piano morphed like guitar
Pushing the limits
Grounded in swing
Always wondered
Why that night
Miles fired him

Jammin' the Jive

Boston Garden
Benefit for
Newport Jazz Festival
On the ropes
After the riot
Entrepreneur George Wein
Not always savvy
Orchestrated jam sessions
Odd juxtapositions
Brubeck on stage
Wein brought out Mingus
Oil and vinegar
Brubeck playing it straight
Academic bop
Jazz Goes to College
Professor Longhair
Without the funk
Mingus being Mingus
Musical comic
Running circles
Round and round
Just hilarious
Cutting Dave
Impish grin
Taking him to school
Like Mozart in Amadeus
Riffing on Salieri
Brilliantly sarcastic
Flat out hilarious
Ended with applause
Mingus awarded

Ears and
This tale
Skewered bull
Once so proud
Hauled off to
Slaughterhouse

Mingus ran circles around Dave Brubeck. Giuliano photo.

Count Basie

During Prohibition
Kansas City wailed
Under Boss Pendergast
President Harry Truman
Played a bit of piano
The Senator from Pendergast
White House
Mobbed up
Tons of saloons
Best of the Midwest
Territory bands
Blues-rooted swing
Charlie Parker
Coleman Hawkins
Andy Kirk
Harland Leonard
Bennie Moten
Major record deal
Young Count Basie
Took over after
Moten and his pal
A physician
Went drinking
Night before procedure
Throat cut
Bled out on the table
Driving around New Haven
Late at night
John Hammond
Yale guy
Old Money

Boola Boola
Heard them on his
Car radio
Visited K.C.
Talked it up
Decca swooped in
Signed Basie
Terrible contract
All his best stuff
Classic sides
Leader as minimalist
Just a few chords
Impeccably placed
Head arrangements
Lester Leaps In
Jumpin' at the Woodside
Goin' To Kansas City
Shorty George
Solid rhythm section
Drummer Joe Jones
Guitar Freddie Green
Keeping the beat
Driving front men
Tenor Lester Young
The Pres
On and off lover
Lady Day
Trumpet Joe Newman
Over the years
So many giants
Moved in and out

Frank Foster's
Shiny Stockings
Backing awesome singers
Jimmy Rushing
Joe Williams
Smack Dab at Newport
Lambert, Hendricks and Ross
Scat set to Basie riffs
Old Blue Eyes
Then late hit
April in Paris
One more time
One more once
Always outrageous
Nobody cut Basie
Jazz royalty
Count outranked Duke
We loved them madly
When jazz was king

Count Basie brought Kansas City blues to his big band. Giuliano photo.

Woody Herman

Igor Stravinsky
Composed
Ebony Concerto
For Woody Herman
Commissioned Dizzy
Woody'n You
Top arrangers for
Best Swing Band
1945 Downbeat poll
End of an era
Disbanded
The next year
One of several changes
Regrouped in '47
Second Herd
Famous for
Horn section
Four Brothers
Zoot Sims, Serge Chaloff
Herbie Steward and Stan Getz
Pushed the envelope
Still toured
Getting on in years
Owed millions to IRS
Caught the gig
Sandy's Jazz Revival
Suburban Beverly
More like a reunion
Drove him back
To Beantown
Quality time

Chauffeur was
All ears
That Sunday
Jazz picnic
Cats hanging out
Jimmy Giuffre
Reeds player
Moody music
Flip Phillips
Yakety yak tenor
Nursing a beer
Host an
Ersatz Gatsby
Dressed like
Sergeant Pepper
With a wig
Wanted to sit in
Grand piano
Huge drum kit
But total jive
Rich kid and his toys
Guys didn't dig him
Sucked on his juice
That was it
Later busted
For fraud
House full of
Leroy Neiman prints
Propped up on
Lucite easels
Burned down

Struck by lightning
Crazy caper
But Woody
Was the real deal

Big band leader Woody Herman. Giuliano photo.

Stan Kenton's Artistry in Rhythm

Tall and lanky
Chiseled features
Slicked-back hair
Elegantly dressed
Double-breasted suit
Still handsome in his 60s
Stan Kenton
Nervous and intense
Strained smile
Touch of the shakes
When we met
For Herald Sunday piece
Less a tour than crusade
Mentor and educator
Reaching a new generation
Schools perform his music
That magnificent
Brassy sound
Some found brash
More noise than jazz
To critics he
Fought with
Trashed his far out
City of Glass
Stan was scrappy
Protective of
Progressive music
Artistry in Rhythm
Afro-Cuban riffs
Singularly magnificent
It was 1970

The year he split
Twenty-five years
With Capital Records
Sides out of print
Kids music he snapped
Referring to the Fab Four
Where before
He was the star
Bought the catalogue
Reissued on his label
Creative World of Stan Kenton
Old and new material
Live albums
Went to all the gigs
Stan glommed onto me
His personal critic
The home guard
Friends and fans
Charlie Lake
The Whale
Spread the word
Whenever in town
Rallied the faithful
Concerts like clinics
Players thrilled
Believed in the music
Famous arrangements
Pete Rugolo, Johnny Richards
Symphonic in scope
Loved the upper register
Red-hot brass

Always new material
Ken Hanna, Neal Hefti, Bill Holman
Macarthur Park a stunner
The band goofing on
Tampico
Hit with June Christy
Other singers
Four Freshmen
Anita O'Day, Chris Conner
Tragically Ann Richards
Posed for Playboy
Wife who knew the band
A suicide at 46
Last time I saw Stan
Staggering to the bus
Knife in my heart
Poignant sight
Another one-nighter
Life on the road
Takes its toll

Buddy Rich

Flashing huge chops
Enormous bebop grin
Buddy Rich
Masterful drummer
Oozed duende
As critic George Frazier
Would say
Slumped on a couch
Tiny cramped
Dressing room
Lennie's on the Turnpike
Latest talk of
Johnny Carson
Perennial guest
Tonight Show
Lennie launched
Another host
Local kid
Doing standup
Jay Leno
Buddy in skivvies
Towel for sweat
Between sets
Always good copy
Covering his gigs
Fronting a big band
Takes bread, balls, charisma
Buddy had it all
Greatest drummer
Of his day
Some say

Challenge from
Max Roach
Winner takes all
Such finesse
Driving the band
Out there
Pirate and highwayman
Moving the sticks
Furiously

Drummer and band leader Buddy Rich. Giuliano photo.

Dizzy

Greatest-ever jazz concert
Massey Hall, Toronto
May 15, 1953
Bird and Diz
Mingus recorded it
Bud Powell dead drunk
Max on drums
Salt Peanuts
Best of bop
Winging it
Post War wail
Cry for freedom
Dizzy bouncing off stage
Checking the fight
Marciano vs. Jersey Joe Walcott
Night of heavyweights
Even Miles
Never topped it
Except for
Kind of Blue
Second-best album
Released six years later
Defining another generation
Then elderly Dizzy
Frequent visitor
No longer
Groovin' High
By then a Báha'í
Fine and mellow
Cheeks puffed out
Like blowfish

Upturned bell
Blistering upper register
Ferocious riffs
Memories of Bird
Dimmed with age
Spin around Boston Harbor
Hanging with hipsters
Cruising and bopping
Hugs for arts elder
Elma Lewis
Gulping salt air
Bop sailor
Lost at sea

Dizzy Gillespie. Giuliano photo.

Mingus Ah Um

Gigs at Jazz Workshop
In for the week
Mingus traveled with
Drummer Danny Richman
Kids from Berklee
Pickup band
Mostly rehearsals
Maybe something
By Saturday night
Now and then
Those amazing bass solos
Pithecanthropus Erectus
My favorite acid music
Next to
Sketches of Spain
Or Sargent Pepper
Those fading barking dogs
Totally wiggy
Always unpredictable
With a big band
Lincoln Center
Mingus got lost
Sheet music too confusing
Tossed it dramatically
Charged on
Head arrangement
Worked through mayhem
Or Boston Garden
Benefit for George Wein
After Newport was trashed
Aretha and Monk

Shoved Mingus onstage
With Dave Brubeck
Apples and oranges
Hilarious as Mingus
Cut Dave to pieces
Like Mozart improvising
A theme by Salieri
Long gone
At Tanglewood
Couple of years back
Gunther Schuller conducted
Reconstructed Mingus composition
Made perfect sense
Great soloists
Missed the funk
Mingus loved Duke
Who fired him
As always
Something else

Old Blue Eyes

Special seats
Three rows added
Over orchestra pit
The Music Hall
Up close and personal
Francis Albert Sinatra
Enjoying Old Blues Eyes
Surrounded by
Mafia royalty
The Patriarca clan
Up from Newport
Favorite singer of
The Dons
Not much left
Of the voice
Impeccable phrasing
Magnificent style
Still swinging tunes
No longer the Kid
From Hoboken
Under the rug
Come Fly with Me
Vegas in Boston
Clicking away
Great shots
Zooming in
Until a Made Man
Turned and said
One more shot kid
I whack you
Omertà for Frank
Offer I could not refuse

Francis Albert Sinatra. Giuliano photos.

Stan Getz

Lush life
Sensual tenor
Stan Getz
Smooth as silk
Ultra complex
Kicked smack
Diverse legacy
Zoot called him
A great bunch of guys
Part of renowned
Four Brothers
On the road
Riding herd
Woody Herman
Peaked with
Samba beat
Brought Bossa Nova
To '60s mainstream
Introduced
Brazilian masters
Antônio Carlos Jobim
Guitarist Luiz Bonfá
Astrud and Joao Gilberto
Iconic hit
Samba standard
The Girl from Ipanema
Grammy for Desafinado
Solid Gold records
Never enough
Got restless
Too confined

Stretched out
Switched horses
As artists do
Fusion with Chick Corea
Band with Gary Burton
Too far out
For the fans
Always solid Stan
True to main man

Stan Getz. Giuliano photo.

Ray Charles and Stevie Wonder

Infield bandstand
Press passes
Up close
Yankee Stadium
Soundblast '66
Pre-Woodstock
Odd program
Opened with
Kid stuff
The McCoys
Can't remember
Strictly filler
Beach Boys
Well OK
Surfer Girl
Sloop John B
Coming to Tanglewood
This summer
Dino rock
Playing Pet Sounds
Brian's masterpiece
The Byrds
Wicked cool
David Crosby
Wearing a cape
Wandering around
Second base
Soul with
The Marvelettes
Up Tight
Everything's All Right

Little Stevie Wonder
Just sixteen
Totally awesome
Grand slam
Dragged off stage
Kicking and screaming
Blowing harmonica
Fading away
Leaving them hungry
One blind brother
Followed by another
Ray Charles anchored
Rocked the stadium
Closing with sing-along
Let's Get Stoned
Reefer madness
Dense cloud over
House that
Ruth built
Over time
Roles reversed
Stevie soared
Reaching ever higher
Still outasight
Charles slid
Off the cliff
Drugs and dames
That late gig
Summer music tent
Phoned it in
Shuck and jive

For squares in
Leisure suits
Rubes in the burbs
Never noticed
Slice and dice
Review
For Patriot Ledger
Broke my heart
Covering decline
Of a giant
Genius of Soul
Down so low

Ray Charles. Giuliano photo.　　Stevie Wonder. Giuliano photo.

Zoot Sims

Melancholy tenor
Low-down swing
Cruising upper register
Stretching out
Rusty tone
Hint of blackberries
Earthy acidity
Lingering on the palate
Tasty chops
Switching to alto
Occasional soprano
Woody Herman Band
Second Herd
Legendary horn section
Four brothers
Three tenors
Zoot, Steward and Getz
Blue Serge
Strung out
On baritone
Bop charts
Zoot Sims
Partnered with
Tenor Al Cohn
Or Mulligan
Baritone like
Boston's Chaloff
From Brothers
Club dates
Lulu White's
Ray Santisi

House piano
Pickup combos
Hanging with Ron
Guest on his
Music America
Passing through
Della Chiesa
Went deep
With those cats
Moody indigo
Shades of black
Dark as night
Deep inside
Where jazz
Knows no color
Other than
Down and dirty
Schmatta
Soiled by life
Beat man
On the road
Veronica's rag
Wiping away
Blood, sweat and tears
Jazz stigmata

Zoot Sims. Giuliano photo.

Gato Barbieri's Last Tango

The Cat
Gato Barbieri
Fused jazz
With Argentine roots
Created music for
Bernardo Bertolucci's
Erotic masterpiece
Anonymous sex
Strangers in a bare pad
Butter scene
Brando and Maria Schneider
Last Tango in Paris
Won a Grammy
Burst of fame
Festival circuit
With signature Fedora
Galvanic on stage
Dance of the gauchos
Flame dimmed
Style morphed
Things change
Since 1985
Monthly gigs
NY's Blue Note
Gutteral attack
From growl to purr
Unique sound
Passionately romantic
Grounded in the pampas
Where they feast
On red meat

Gato Barbieri recorded sound track to *Last Tango in Paris*. Giuliano photo.

Janis Joplin's Last Gig

Rock star
Janis Joplin
Texas blues belter
Hanging in Frisco
Performed live
August 12, 1970
At Harvard Stadium
Packed to the gills
Not long after
October 4
To be exact
Stone cold dead
Nodded out on smack
Smashed her face
Nose broken
Shoved into her brain
What a way to go
Kids were restless
That summer
Revolution in the air
Street fighting man
Concert series
Meant to take edge off
Not really dude
As things turned out
Show was late
Something about
Stolen equipment
Me in hippy gear
Stoked like the crowd
Reefer madness

Covering for
Boston Herald Traveler
Straight gig
Old Yankee rag
Janis was swigging
Southern Comfort
Her Mother Courage
Fans getting restless
Burst on stage
Raunchy ad-lib
About getting stoned
Turning tricks
Bootleg LP
Caught it all
Short set
Just eight songs
Tell Mama
Half Moon
Mercedes Benz
My Baby
Try
Maybe
Summertime
Full Tilt
Left them hungry
Just a taste
Streaming out
Raising hell
Fans trashed
Harvard Square
Bricks through

Plateglass windows
Striking a blow
For freedom
Wrote one of several
Rock obits
Hendrix, Morrison, Joplin
Looking back
At wasted youth
Anthems for
Rows of names
Purple Haze
Vietnam Memorial
Turbulent days
When nothing seemed
Right with the world

Tenor Titan Sonny Rollins

Jammed up young
Stint at Rikers
Hooked on horse
In and out with Miles
Kicked early
Now mid-eighties
Last of the Titans
Pillars of jazz
Tenor colossus
Sonny Rollins
Staggering legacy
Flailing his horn
Bobbing and weaving
A weapon
On the attack
Turning mostly
Mundane tunes
Into scorching riffs
Deconstructing
Chord changes
Often improv more on
Rhythm than melody
First to downscale
Quartet to trio
Ditched the piano
Collaborations
Cliff Brown/ Max Roach
Horn player Brown
Car accident
Bright light
Snuffed

Several sabbaticals
Woodshedding
Pushing the limits
Returned as
The Bridge
Magnificently
Black rage of
Freedom Suite
Flip side playful
Way out West
Pratfalls with MJQ
Loosey-goosey
Goofing on their
Sedate chamber music
Just hilarious
More jab than jive
Always a surprise
Roaming the stage
Balletic moves
Sweeping reach
Accenting the beat
At Tanglewood
Not long ago
Hobbled with age
Arthritic bones
No impact on
Feline sound
Scorching growls
Rough and smooth
Laid down
A groove

Sonny Rollins. Giuliano photos.

Madam Bricktop

Then in her 80s
Cabaret singer
From Paris
Hostess of Lost Generation
Madam Bricktop
So named for red hair
Legacy of Irish father
Negro mother
Worked Chitlin' Circuit
Theater Owners Booking Circuit
AKA to entertainers as
Tough on black asses
Escaped prejudice
Sailed to France
Like Bechet and Baker
Sang Miss Otis Regrets
Slow and articulate
Enunciating lyrics
Cole Porter wrote for her
Rusty pipes
Ancient timbre
Legendary artist
Tall and frail
Elegant moves
That night at
Lulu White's
In Boston's South End
Still vivid
Timeless bubbles
Dom Perignon
Life's champagne

So intoxicating
Like 50 ccs of
Paris air
Captured in a flask
By Duchamp
When Dada longed
For Mama
Over There

Madam Bricktop entertained the Lost Generation in Paris. Giuliano photo.

Lady Day

Signature gardenias
In her hair
Perfume accenting
Sweet scent of
That lilting voice
Unique texture
Fractured and cracked
Ravaged by racism
Strung out on junk
Narrow range
Not great pipes
Rusted by life
Impeccable phrasing
Laying back
Wafted by beat
Consummate swing
Teddy Wilson on piano
Laying down the bones
Of tunes
God Bless the Child
Most harrowing
Strange Fruit
Sobbed when first heard
Choked up ever since
Thinking of the
Scent of magnolias
In the gallant South
Burning flesh
Twisted mouth
Easter Weekend in
Natchez

Mississippi Goddamn
Ghosts like
Spanish moss
Hanging from the
Poplar trees
Lady Day
Grew up with
Lester Young
Friend and lover
It's complicated
She called him Prez
Like Duke, Count, King and Earl
Royalty of jazz
His mellow horn
Scorched with pain
After the Army
Spirit broken in the brig
Their suffering
Down and mellow
Speaking to our
Hearts and minds
Setting the bar
For art and humanity
Above and beyond
That bridge too far

Duh Ramones

Motorcycle jackets
Torn jeans
Punk rockers
America's Sex Pistols
Four guys from
Forest Hills, Queens
Not related
Joey, Johnny, Dee Dee, Tommy
Ramones
Gabba Gabba Hey
Fed up with rock
Too commercial
Overproduced
Back to basics
One, Two, Three, Four
Hey Ho Let's Go
Straight ahead
Short sets
Two-minute songs
Like it used to be
Those 45s
Singles they loved
Grew up on
Buddy Holly
Chuck Berry
Knew four chords
Slammed them home
Blistering speed
Blitzkrieg Bop
No fancy stuff
Joey in a stance

Choking the mike
Endless gigs
Downtown scene
Max's and CBGB's
Twenty years
Constant touring
Never chart busters
Adored by critics
Tons of albums
Couple of films
Even that monster
Phil Spector
Got a piece of them
Wall of sound
Like the Ronettes
Put a gun to Joey's head
Spector offed his
Girlfriend
What a creep
End of the Century
Biggest near hit
Johnny debunked it
Not the real Ramones
Fights and feuds
Band members
Came and went
Shuffled in and out
Final show
August 6, 1996
Not long after
No easy retirement

By 2001 three dead
Tommy in 2014
Rock 'n' Roll Hall of Fame
Some say
Next to the Beatles
Greatest rock band
Of all time
No shit

Johnny Ramone. Giuliano photo.

Ella Fitzgerald

Just a kid
Talent night at the Apollo
Off the hook
Rocked Harlem
Then the world
Broke out with
Drummer Chick Webb
Big band era
He died young at 34
Her novelty hit
A-Tisket, A-Tasket
A brown and yellow basket
That was 1938
When Swing was King
She was 21
Never looked back
First Lady of Song
Soaring to stratosphere
Scat out of hell
Untouchable
Nudged and challenged
Bested her friend
Sarah Vaughan
Cutting contests
Ella reaching higher
Always inventive
Porgy and Bess
With Satchmo
Called him Pops
Oil and vinegar
Top chops

Even when messing up
Out there improv
Like Mack the Knife
Live in Berlin
Forgetting lyrics
Faking them
Over the top
Ella and Duke at the Côte D'Azur
With legend Coleman Hawkins
You wanted her to
Screw up
Ella's special mojo
Always at her best
Radiant warmth
Infectious humor
Incredible invention
Less so in later gigs
Superb but melancholy
Thick glasses
So many operations
Heart wrenching
Those final festivals
Poignant memories
Such a great artist
Class to the max
Caught on wax
But not waning
In Hall of Fame

Ella Fitzgerald. Giuliano photos.

Scat Singer Annie Ross

Three schoolboys
Storyville
1950s digging
Lambert, Hendricks and Ross
Nursing Shirley Temples
Acting cool
Hormones raging
Fixated on
Galvanic Annie Ross
Swinging in
Red satin sheath
Elbow length
White gloves
Like Lady Day
Hiding tracks
Ripping scat
Vocalese masters
Voices like horns
Lester Leaps In
Jumpin' at the Woodside
Goin' to Kansas City
All the Basie riffs
Blistering speed
Blur of lyrics
Cloudburst
Early on
Duets with legendary
King Pleasure
Solo with Mulligan
I Feel Pretty
Backed by baritone

Growling blend
Rough and smooth
Sent me to heaven
Teen lust
Rare Boston gig
Decades later
Returned to London
Awesome icon
Surviving outrageous
Era of jazz supreme

Annie Ross. Giuliano photo.

Sarah Vaughan

Another talent night
Harlem's iconic
Apollo Theater
Sarah Vaughan won
Ten bucks
Plus opening for Ella
In 1943
Friends and rivals
From then on
Big band era
Matter of taste
Three jazz divas
Billie, Ella and Sarah
They called her Sassy
Unique style
Remarkable range
Impeccable swing
Perfect timing
Full of feeling
Early on
Slender and sexy
Sustained vibrato
Working the guts
Out of songs
Misty to
Send in the Clowns
Music for lovers
Duets with Eckstein
Utter classics
Often however
Over produced

Mercury Records
In the '50s
Swamped by strings
Too commercial
They all did
Billie to Dizzy
Even Bird
Later on
When I caught her
Festival circuit
Matronly by then
Pure jazz
Ripping through
Audiences riveted
By her passion
Making her for some
Number one

Sarah Vaughan. Giuliano photo.

Betty Bop

Jazz singer
Betty Carter
Queen of scat
Vocalese
Betty Bop
Pulled and stretched
Lyrics bounced around
More moves than
Harlem Globetrotters
Trick shots
Fiddled and diddled
Three pointers
Half court zingers
Standards sliced and diced
Bobbing and weaving
Fade away jumpers
Pyrotechnics
Started with Satchmo
The Hot Five
Heebie Jeebies
Claimed he forgot
Made it up
The great imposter
Inventor of jazz
Told Alan Lomax
Why I myself
Mr. Jelly Roll Morton
Did indeed invent
Scat singing
Piano man in a cathouse
Down in New Orleans

What does scat mean
Lomax asked
Library of Congress
Recordings
Why scat ain't nothin'
But what gives a song
Some flavor
Kindah like this
Diddidah doo
Dewop scaddah wham
If you'ze hip
To the jive

Scat singer Betty Carter. Giuliano photo.

Carmen McRae

Small club
Between sets
Hanging with
Carmen McRae
Explained
Respect for lyrics
Selling a song
Lean and mean
Straight no chaser
Taking it low
Easy and slow
Pulling out
The scenario
Meticulous
Articulation
Never rushed
Total command
Crisp clarity
Cabaret style
American songbook
Show tunes
Jazz gumbo
Swept along
Infectious swing
Making our
Hearts sing
Even at
Symphony Hall
Festival gig
Still felt
So close

Poignant and personal
Meant
As if
Just for me

Carmen McRae. Giuliano photo.

Pixie Voiced Cabaret Singer

Blossom Dearie
That incredible name
So perfect for
Such a fragrant
Flower
Skipping lightly
Through a tulip field
Hip and playful
Lyrics with an edge
Shockingly sophisticated
A tad off-color
All the more astonishing
From such a wispy
Girlish voice
Best consumed
Up close and personal
Debonair setting
Supper clubs
Master of cabaret
Asked her about
Legendary King Pleasure
Such a mystery
Greatest of all
Scat singers
Super Fly
1952 duet
Iconic tune
Moody's Mood for Love
Perfect synergy
Hot and cool
Sweet and sour

Rare opportunity
One who was there
Actually knew him
Not much was
Disappointing answer
Just hired for session
Made jazz history
Flashpoint
Pleasure just slithered
Into the mist
Enveloping
Fog of time

Cabaret singer Blossom Dearie. Giuliano photo.

Great American Songbook

More than a century
Broadway Musicals
Those great shows
Carousel
South Pacific
King and I
Sound of Music
My Fair Lady
Cabaret
West Side Story
Standards of
Great American Songbook
Archived now
Performing Arts Center
Carmel, Indiana
Initiative of Michael Feinstein
Preserving a legacy
In the vaults
Live onstage
Magnificent theater
Sweet-voiced
Barbara Cook
Now in her 80s
Joined him
Giving new meaning
To Sondheim
Up close and personal
Sharing insights
Sweeping us
Back in time
At Tanglewood

That summer
Liza took the train
Up from the Apple
Invited onstage
Another senior
Belted out
That anthem
New York, New York
If you can make it there
You can make it anywhere
Thrilling audiences
Enriching a heritage
So full of Americana
No business
Like show business
Celebrating
Great White Way

Barbara Cook. Giuliano photo.

Lou Reed

The Times today
Review of Lou Reed
Bio by Howard Sounes
Some fucker
Looking for a buck
Trash Talk
Monster myth
Truth or dare
Who cares
Only for the famous
Or nearly so
Nobody remembers
The peccadilloes
Of you and me
Just average blokes
Not like Bush
Bone-headed boob
Faking it during
Vietnam
National Guard Holiday
All those scams
We all have them
Not big time
Changing the course
Of history
Other than our own
Soft tales
Played out in verse
To amuse ourselves
Perhaps a few others
Better to rehash

Crazed tormented souls
Artists crying out
For our sins
Unable to save themselves
Or even a dog
Rescued from
Burning buildings
Of self
Rest with no peace
In graves dug
By rock'n'roll

Lou Reed. Giuliano photo.

Lou Two

That Dante night
St. Marks Place
Renee Ricard
Decadent poet hustler
My Vergil
The Dom
Exploding Plastic Inevitable
He kicked the giant ball
Velvet Underground
Nico on vocals
The G doing his whip dance
In leather pants
Don't fit no more
Taking a walk
On the wild side
All those times since
Over and over
Steve and the
Woodrose Ballroom
Woven in
Press conference
Years later
Hosted by
Don Delacey and RCA
Gone solo
Almost famous
Snarled at us
Drank bottle of
Courvoisier
In an hour
Afternoon before

Sloppy staggering gig
All style no substance
Before he went clean
So we're told
Like Laurie's gig
At Mass MoCA
With Lou on a leash
I asked him about
Jonathan Richman and
The Modern Lovers
He worshiped Lou
Reed just scoffed
Snapped out of stupor
Zapped a zinger
Killed the messenger
In Dublin
Learned of his death
The Irish press
Seemed so odd
How legends end
I read the news today
Oh boy

Modern Lovers

Free Sunday concerts
Cambridge Common
Kid from Natick
Solo act
Jonathan Richman
Short hair
Blasting mantra
I'm Straight
Kind of a goof
Left for the Apple
Hung with
Velvet Underground
Worshiped Lou
After swigging
Bottle of Courvoisier
Pretty smashed
Asked him about
Modern Lovers
Lou just laughed
Told Jonathan
Shocked he asked
Lou said that
1973 neighbor Arthur Gallagher
Fallon Place
Hippie enclave
Looking for a band
College Week spring break
Family hotel
Inverurie in Bermuda
A few kids came
Next night
Back with more

Became fans
Tourism supported
Picnics on the beach
Local band
Bermuda Strollers
Wings of a Dove
We heard them
Day after day
At night
Helping to set up
Kind of promoter
And roadie
Jerry Harrison's
Electric keyboard
Dave Robinson's drums
Ernie Brooks on bass
Classic Modern Lovers
Roadrunner
Massachusetts anthem
She Cracked
Jonathan always
Insecure and nerdy
Reflecting on why
Nobody Called
Pablo Picasso
An Asshole
After a week
Lovers wicked tight
Got them a gig
Sandy's
A scorcher
In and out of studios

Revolving door
Producers and demos
Jonathan ever restless
Wanted new sound
Softer more acoustic
Hand clapping
No more Velvets
Robinson joined
The Cars
Later Harrison
Split for Talking Heads
Brooks played with
David Johansen, Elliot Murphy
Jonathan well
Still Jonathan
Something About Mary
Cult following
Now middle aged
Adolescent

Left to right David Robinson, Jonathan Richman and Gerry Harrison. Photo by Steve Nelson.

DJ Ron Della Chiesa

Spinning platters
Weaving tales
Guest of DJ
Ron Della Chiesa
Music America
Hanging out
Boogie nights
Lulu White's
Scarfing up
Willard Chandler's
Tasty gumbo
Digging the sounds
When jazz abounded
Best of Beantown
Fenton Hollander's
Harbor cruises
Making waves
Up at Sandy's
Far frontier
Of hipness
In Beverly
After legendary
Lennie's on the Turnpike
Went up in smoke
That gonzo scene
In Cambridge
With bon vivant
Martin Slobodkin
Out there man
Ask Ron about it
Started with WBCN

Wacko owner
Pioneer of FM
T. Mitchell Hastings
Program director
Organized playlist
Fast, medium, slow
That didn't work
Then all religious
Before the station
Famously went
Total rock
By then Ron
Ensconced at WGBH
When late fellow DJ
Robert J. Lurtsema
Called Ron
Instructions to
Start the birds
Perhaps this summer
We'll catch up at
Newport or Tanglewood
The cat still swings
Remembering when
Jazz was king

Music America host Ron Della Chiesa. Giuliano photo.

Amy and Tony Body and Soul

Whom the gods love
Last session
Amy Winehouse
Just twenty-seven
Awed by the master
Raspy voiced
Tony Bennett
Spanning generations
Irony that he survived
To swing another day
While by then
Ravaged by love
Flesh ripped from bones
Everyone wanted a
Piece of her
Skittish and scared
Running on vapors
Stepped back
Devastated at
Messing the take
Confidence collapsed
Ready to bolt
Gently he nursed her
Through it
After a pause
Another try
Wrenched up from
Inferno
Blues from
Lower depths
Shattering sound

Ninth circle
Bottom of hell
Body and soul
Harrowing glimpse
Of that session
From the documentary
Breaking down
Edge of collapse
She told him
With laser honesty
I've never done this before
Don't think I can
There with her idol
Artist she worshiped
Grew up on
Reaching back
One more time
Whiffing chin music
Brushing back Tony
Leaning inside
Braced for high heat
Rock steady
Solid foundation
Took his cut
Her passion
Clinging to his
Confidence
Coaxing greatness
The best from her
Staggering the senses
Paparazzi flames

Incinerated
A fragile Phoenix
Broken bird
Trampled by fame
Reborn in our
Hearts and minds
Remembering
Tony said
She was really a great jazz singer
A true jazz singer
And I regret that
Because that's the 'right way' to sing

Tony Bennett. Giuliano photo.

Peter Wolf

Heart and soul
Boston's Wolf Man
With artist Paul Shapiro
On guitar
Hallucinations
First DJ
When WBCN
Went rock
Midnight from Tea Party
Ooffa woofa
Wamma jamma
Beautiful tragic Edie
Later J Geils Band
Mario the Big M
Discovered them
Blue-eyed soul
Signed with Atlantic
Heavy hitter
Frank Barsalona
Manager
Over the top
They broke up
Bad vibes
Peter hosted
Muddy Waters
Birthday party
Blues master
Mother to us all
Passing through
Mississippi via Chicago
Neighbor in the

Murder Building
University Road
Harvard Square
Encountering
Annie Leibovitz
In from Frisco
Shooting him for
Rolling Stone
When not on the road
Through the alley
Past Casa B
And Harvest
To Cardell's
For breakfast
Faye Dunaway
The lady made demands
Introduced him
Pip this is Peter
Peter this is Pip
Sister swooned
So long ago

Peter Wolf. Giuliano photo.

Jimi Hendrix RIP and Read

Exquisite corpses
Dead so young
Just 27
Both in London
Amy Winehouse
Jimi Hendrix
Decades apart
Similar drift
Total genius
Burned at both ends
Out out brief candle
Came over the wire
RIP and read
News flash
Landed on my desk
Boston Herald Traveler
1970 Rookie Year
Writing obits
First Al Wilson
Jim Morrison
Bathtub in Paris
How poetic
Covered Joplin's last gig
Harvard Stadium
Followed by riots
Overdosed not long after
Recently another binge
Swing of
Grim Reaper
Talking 'bout my generation
Bowie, Glenn Frey, Keith Emerson

Comes in bunches
So it seems
My age more or less
Plus or minus 75
Keith of the Stones
Still standing
Against all odds
The Living Dead
Thinking of Jimi
Saved that wire
Stuck in a folder
All these years
Yellowed with time
Not meant to last
Not Fade Away
Who needs
Yesterday's newspapers
Mick asked
Me I guess
Thinking back to
Cheetah in the '60s
Hangin' out
Curtis Knight and the Flames
Broadway soul band
Nothing special
Mustang Sally
Fake leopard skin shirts
Frederick's of Hollywood
Backstage Curtis said
You guys be out front tonight
Turning Jimi loose

All those licks
Lightning struck
Branded by memory
Photographer Gerry Berkerey
Mentor and I
Visited flophouse
Front desk shouted
Jimi you got guests
Oddly shy
Fishy handshake
Street clothes
We gave him pictures
Long since lost
Known then as
Jimi James
Left for London
In a Village pad
House of Blues
Good smoke
Lava lamps
Gerry Sherman
College pal
Lives in Amsterdam
Had all the new sounds
High as a kite
Wacky weed
In the dark of night
Fresh vinyl
Jimi Hendrix Experience
Knew that guitar
Listened intently

Studied the cover
Could it be
Gone Mod
The same dude
Woodstock
Electric Ladyland
Changed everything
Like Robert Johnson
Me and the Devil
Was walking side by side
You may bury my body, ooh
down by the highway side
So my old evil spirit
can catch a Greyhound bus and ride
Irony that
The last Hendrix gig
Boston Common
Never happened
Ashes to ashes
Lust to dust

Marc Bolan's Pratfall

Touted as bigger
Than the Beatles
T. Rex
Glam-rocker Marc Bolan
Mickey Finn on percussion
Early 1970s
Eleven top-ten British hits
T. Rextasy they called it
Set to storm America
Hyped as second coming
Big time PR firm
Shuffled us in and out
Fifteen minutes each
Media face time
Me and the other lads
Warned to be nice
To Marc he being
So sensitive poetic and
Bollocks
First night of tour
Boston gig
Press en masse
Poised for rock history
Curtain parted
Marc hopped on stage
Hit a chord
Skip and flourish
Bang a Gong (Get It On)
Fell flat on his ass
Brutal reviews
Tour bombed

Band slipped off charts
Marc and girlfriend
Wrapped short
Around tree
Way too young
British rocker
Exquisite corpse
Dead as that
Dinosaur T. Rex
All teeth
Frightful beast

Cyndi Lauper

Interacting
Reaching out
Clasping hands
With fans
The young
Cyndi Lauper
Girl just wanted
To have fun
Hint of what
Was to come
Time After Time
Haunting ballad
Miles recorded
His horn
Caressing the melody
Lovely tune
Richly evocative
Surprising accolade
Decades later
Tony for
Kinky Boots
From punk babe
To Broadway
Talented girl
Matured nicely
Enduring artist
Formidable woman
Not fade away
Here to stay

Cyndi Lauper. Giuliano photo.

Black Star

Ever morphing
David Bowie
Chameleon
Multiple personas
Androgynous
Lithe and thin
Slithering lizard
Ever lethal
Riveting riffs
Shed like
Snakeskins
Ashes to ashes
Through life
Always evolving
Look and style
Finest artist
Of his generation
Widely imitated
Beyond compare
Even in death
Space oddity
Major Tom
Time-warped
Messages from
That space
Beyond
Gravity bound
Mother Earth
Waves of sound
Sonic boom
Hauntingly ethereal

De Profundis
Black Star
Final opus
Rock requiem
Last testament
Dark and pixelated
Brooding
Image deconstructed
From a stadium
World tour
When with bravado
He asked us
To dance
How macabre
We shuffle to a
Terminal assault
Invading our senses
Gut wrenching
Lasting legacy
Challenging
Strangely
Beyond comprehension
In every dimension
For those who
Dare to dream

Illinois Jacquet

Long before
Yakety yak sax
Clarence Clemons'
Black Bottom
Springsteen's E Street
Trane's altissimo
Overblowing
Pushing his tenor
To heroic upper
Registers
Early on Texas horn
Honk master
Illinois Jacquet
Nee Jean Baptiste
From Louisiana actually
Creole and Indian
Started with alto
Lionel Hampton
Switched him to tenor
Just a kid
First recording
One take
Eighty-second solo
May 26, 1942
Flying Home
Riff a classic in
Berklee fake books
Hamp wore him out
Cab Calloway then
Trio with Mingus
Later Basie and Ella

Hit the road
Jazz at the Philharmonic
All-star jam sessions
Captured on vinyl
Entrepreneur
Norman Granz
Unique sound
So memorable
Rough and crude
Angry growl
Compared to
Bird's soaring solos
Mixing it up
With boppers
Gigs at Lulu White's
Boston's South End
Named for NOLA
Cathouse in
Storyville
Where jazz was born
Chef Chandler
Slinging the gumbo
Ron always ringside
Hanging with sidekicks
Illinois versatile
All the horns
Richly textured rarity
Blues bassoon
Swinging the night away
Sweet and sassy

Illinois Jacquet. Giuliano photo.

OMG

Oops
Sorry sorry sorry
In a frenzy
Down and dirty
Rattled and frazzled
Mea Culpa
My bad
Ruddy wanker
Muggahfuggah
Cheesed off
Fuggeddahbouit
Flippin crappy
Shit fit
It slipped
Big time
Huge
As Pip would say
Back in the day
When hell
Freezes over
Nightmare
Cold sweat
Please Please Please
Senior moment
Shit happens
Dude
I'll make it up
To you
Promise
On my honor
Next time

My dime
Later man
Ground control
To major Tom
Cripes
How I miss
Bowie
Lazarus
His finale
Exquisite corpse
Ziggy
Stardust
Ashes to ashes
Total
Cluster fuck

That's me, top row, second from the right.

First Communion

Nuns prepared us
First communion
Taking in the Lord
The Holy Host
Etiquette involved
Swallow don't chew
Tasted like wheat
Not gluten free
Think pious thoughts
To and from altar
Instant state of grace
Practiced with Necco wafers
Taking turns being priest
Prior to confession
What's a sin
I wanted to know
When in the booth
Door sliding open
Bless you my son
Pouring out sins
Mostly venial
Just everyday stuff
Making it up
No big deal
Not mortal ones like
Rape and murder
Heavens not that
Being mean
Impure thoughts
Self-abuse
Hard to understand

Sounded interesting
Angels not looking
Gave it a wank
Handy to confess
Priests understand
When you come clean
It all goes away
Liked that idea
Confessing
Ever since
No matter what
Penance always the same
Five Our Fathers
Five Hail Marys
Blurted out
Quick as can be
Got boring
Upped the ante
Beat my sister
Killed the dog
No change
Robbed a bank
Same old same old
Five and Five
How Catholics
Get away with murder
Tell the priest
Let him worry
What they do
Just between me
Guy in the booth
God only knows

Econo Class

Back from Europe
Cheap flight
She said
Half price
Real cheap
Just $500
Round-trip
How was it
Well, not so great
No food
No entertainment
All one class
Tight squeeze
Paid for water
Coin-operated
Restrooms
A Euro
Extra for bags
One carry-on
Cost for Wi-Fi
Charged for overweight
Came to a fortune
No free snacks
Brought sandwiches
Last minute
Passed the hat
For fuel
To land
Getting there
Not half the fun

Pathfinder

Born in slums
An everyman
Anytime anywhere
Left for frontier
Hacked through forest
Created clearing
Built a cabin
Hunting and trapping
Winters hunkered down
Summers tending gardens
Grew corn and squash
Took a native woman
Raised their children
Living well
In harmony with
Mother Earth
Then they came
A trickle at first
Cabins here and there
Became a village
Then a town
Eventually a city
Finally yet again
Poverty and brutality
Where once was
Pristine wilderness
Too late to leave
Perhaps in dream
Another planet
Starting over

Peacemaker

Just a kid
His dad dead
Shiloh they said
Shot in the head
By Johnny Reb
Headed west
Rousting about
First one self-defense
Bar brawl
Spilled to street
Happened in a flash
Didn't know the guy
Watched him die
Then another and another
Never liked the killing
Came with a rush
Never more alive
Some clean one bullet
Others messy bleeding out
Strangers came to town
Gunning for him
Tested his speed
The last barely twenty
Short and mean
Cut down
That was it
Walked away
Wife and kids
Working fields
Got him with a rifle
Cheat shot from

Behind the ridge
They say son of
Man he killed
Years prior
Then someone
Got him
All that before
War to end all wars
Over there

Bookends

IIn the lobby
Snacks and drinks
Perhaps Earl Gray tea
Waiting for the show
A dramatic comedy
Theatre in the Berkshires
Found a seat
Arriving early
Just chilling
Between two couples
Elderly and infirm
Swapping symptoms
Describing procedures
Remember so and so
Lou Gehrig's
A doctor no less
Nothing to be done
Hobbling about
Between here and Florida
Years of commuting
Tales of
Global travel
India was great but
Bad air in Beijing
Been just about everywhere
The usual audience
No sign of kids
Can't afford it
Not so young myself
Laundry list of
Pills and pains

This for that
Thinking ahead
How long before
Just like them
Perhaps never
Not my style
Or so I think
Still in the pink

Siesta to Semester

As a kid
Shocked by
Back-to-school
Window displays
Brown's Department Store
Downtown Gloucester
Mid-August
How could that be
Still summer it
Seemed to me
Later teaching college
Out by May
Fourth of July
Sense of dread
Vacation half gone
Counting the days
Fall semester
Started with faculty lunch
Annual convocation
President Sargent
Long past his prime
Still earning millions
That boilerplate
Inspirational speech
Faculty in robes
What a snooze
Starting classes
Fresh student rosters
First lectures
Too many courses
Long commutes

Late nights followed by
Early mornings
End of first week
Totally pooped
Too soon frazzled
Now oblivious to
All that stress
Endless vacation
Phasing into
Life's winter season
When they grant
No degrees

Saints

Saints preserve us
What does that mean
Praying to slivers
Fragments of martyrs
Slaughtered in
Gruesome ways
Broken on the wheel
Stretched on the rack
Burned at the stake
The lucky ones
Hanged or beheaded
Hacked up with chainsaws
Mafia style
Like Gotti's neighbor
Ran over his kid
Accident pure and simple
How does all that
Misfortune relate to us
Praying to saints
Pilgrimages to churches
Votive offerings cluttering altars
Crutches and canes
Detritus of cures
Saved by miracles
Bad luck of saints
While heaven knows
Day to day wonders
Nothing short of miraculous

First Light

Necktie party
At dawn
Condemned man
Ordering last meal
Make that a
Two-pound boiled lobster
Starter of steamers
With drawn butter
Baked potato
Apple pie and ice cream
Meeting with priest
Guard brought in
Big Mac with large fries
Hey prisoner cried
I'm gluten free
Doctor told me
Cut back on fat
Avoid complex carbs
Oh well said the screw
How about last cigarette
Gave up smoking
First light
Crept into cell
Swig of Diet Coke
That'll kill you
For sure
Reverend said
Sorry about the
Gallows humor
Better to laugh
Than cry

Troy

Insulted
Arrogant Achilles
Sulked in his tent
Killed Hector
Bravest of Trojans
Dragged corpse
Around walls
Unrepentant hubris
Wailing women
His father Priam
Pleaded for
Ravaged body
Rites of burial
Mighty warrior
Slain and defamed
Yet again hero
Dark poet of Greeks
Most radiant of men
Rallied tide of battle
Routing the enemy
So many ships
Beached on the shore
Ten years on
Away from home
Their boys now men
From afar
Guided by Apollo
Arrow of Paris
Abductor of Helen
Pretty boy and coward
Found its target

Brought down
Cities named for him
In France and Texas
Nowhere in the world
One named for
Mighty Achilles
No great city just
Remembered for
Heel

Ancient Warriors.

Contrarian

Given all kinds of
Fine advice
Well intended
To be sure
For your own good
How to do it better
They insist
Try this or that
Change the last line
Consider another way
Be like them
Follow the herd
Seen and heard
Hard of herding
Share their values
They implore
Worship same gods
Or ideas
Don't listen
Shrug it off
Deaf as a post
Ears waxed shut
Stubborn as heck
Downright contrarian
No rules or regulations
Follow different path
One less taken
Fork in the road
Heaven or Hell
Not making sense
Don't really matter

Lead your own life
Take my advice
Or better not
If you know
What's good
From me
With no regrets

Fall

Fall came early
August actually
Markets fell
Plunged like a stone
Deep into sea of
Global anxiety
Ruined vacations
Lazy days
Beaches of world
Sand in pants
Crabs nipping at heels
Tranquility roiled
Empty nest eggers
Calling brokers
Calmly stated
No worries
Sit tight
Just a correction
All is well
Mighty China
Seeming more
Like Greece
On the skids
Taking us down
Storm clouds
Shadows over
Last days of summer

Bonsai

Worked
Herald Traveler
Back in 1975
Evening commute
On a whim
Purchased houseplant
Flower shop in the subway
Member of ficus family
Revived through
Near death experiences
Disease and neglect
Finally terminal
Sticky scale
Leaves a mess
One last attempt
Total triage
Leaves removed
Pruned to a stump
Root ball reduced
Soil replaced
Forced growth
Miraculous recovery
Green and shiny
Last rays of summer
Back inside
Another winter
Ancient companion
Gnarled and complex
Forty years
Illustrating journey
Secret life of plants

Boston

Death in Boston
Not like Venice
Brahmins
Strolling Back Bay
Come and go
Praising Michelangelo
Cabots speak
Only to Lowells
At the Algonquin
On Comm Ave
While in Southie
Whitey dines at
Amrheins
Speaking only
To God

Unequivocal

Regarding the matter at hand
Which is despicable
By any measure of decency
Although opinions vary
As well they should
Meaning no disrespect
Even though
Hard to see how
Right-minded person
Could be so stupid
This being a free society
For which patriots
Fought and died
To protect rights
For differences
However nonsensical
Expressed by the
Well-intended
Strong beliefs
However misguided
Our society
Allows for diversity
Must be respected
Within limits
Reasonable doubt
Strongly agree
To disagree

Kicks

After the Beatles
On Ed Sullivan
Had to have
Spanish boots
Crystal's in Combat Zone
Crazy kicks
Catering to pimps
Snake, alligator, ostrich
Beatle boots
Looked so cool
Thin soles
Split at the sides
Endless trips
To cobbler
Foot fetish
Phil's in the South End
Sold seconds
Matched them
Ten bucks a pair
Mostly samples
One of a kind
Groovy platforms
Pink pumps
With codpiece pants
Phyllis designed
Hanging at Newport
Smiles of a summer night
Things change
Now just one pair
Lasts years
Docksiders

Well worn
Falling apart
Bennington outlet
Astrid bought shoes
Durable and sleek
More walking around
Than slip and slide
All that jive
Done gone down

Subway Sirens

Underground
The T in Boston
Symphony stop
Ancient and grimy
Waiting on bench
Staring at stained walls
Looking back
Ann Taylor diptych
Paired images
Same girl
Pretty but generic
Chic clothes
For working girls
Who actually work
As well as play
In these outfits
The eyes radiate
On the left hauteur
The other panel
Brooding vulnerability
The gaze coached
Twenty-somethings
With attitude
For the camera
Not much behind
Ersatz angst
Getting paid
Quite well in fact
To sell stuff
Before nips and tucks
Put them

Out of business
Followed by the next
Fine-boned girl
From Kansas
While it lasts
Billboard queens
Seducing commuters

Underground advertising on the MBTA.

Old Miss

Finally
Old Miss
Gave up state flag
Banned from campus
Confederate heritage
Dies hard
Visiting Natchez
Easter weekend
How ironic
Death and resurrection
Gracious mansions
Built by slaves
Beautiful but horrific
Black rage
Beneath the surface
Contempt from waiter
Slapping down food
Southern hospitality
Scent of magnolias
Burning flesh
Memory of lash
Boy fetch me
This or that
Make it quick y'all
If you be so kind
Nina's anthem
Wrenching our guts
Now more than ever
Mississippi Goddam

Dr. Nutt, who built Longwood in Natchez, owned hundreds of slaves.

High Bush

Work gets harder
Takes time
More spread out
Low-hanging fruit
The anecdotes
Easy stories
Picked clean
Reaching higher
Takes a ladder
My consigliore
Brother Robert
Main man
Explained it
Like Cuban cigars
Finest in the world
Perfect climate
Soil and humidity
Rare tobacco
Bottom leaves
The filler
Rolled not chopped
Middle leaves
Binder around them
Upper leaves
Baked by the sun
Delicate transparent
The wrapper
Gives the flavor
Tender and moist
Rolled with one's fingers
Savoring aroma

Kissed by flame
Filling mouth
Wafting up nose
Paired with V.S.O.P.
Treasured contraband
Banned in U.S.A.
Fruit of Castro's
Forbidden revolution
Taboo topics
Shared by comrades
Private clubs
Or rustic huts
Explorers
Staggering in from
Terra incognita
Telling tales
Caves of Tibet
Frozen tundra
Mountain retreat
Hassan's assassins
Trance-like reverie
Conjuring esoteric
Bursting flavors
Sweat lodge initiates
Moby Dick survivors
Pineapples of hospitality
Marooned memories

Moby Dick

Call me Ishmael
Read too young
Craved adventure
Fantasy of possibilities
Cowboys and Indians
Lewis and Clark
Pirates of the Caribbean
Whaling in Pacific
Those great characters
Sailing from Nantucket
The white whale
One-legged Ahab
Full of rich detail
Sharing stash of
Shrunken heads
Shivered imagination
Later college professor
Moby Dick as God
Battle of good and evil
Not seeing
Deconstructed content
Books read for pleasure
Deeply probed
Pulled apart
Studied and sifted
Sanguine thirst
For global adventures
Never happened
Worked for a living
No South Sea Islands
Other than imagination

Nightly entertainment
Pretty vacant
Then sleep
Perchance to dream
God and dead whales
Lost Neverland

Whale off Nantucket. Giuliano photo.

Sirens

Like brave Ulysses
Voyage home
Youth squandered in Troy
Folly of glory
Should I plug my ears
Like the men
Tied to the mast
Of public opinion
Passing rugged shore
Dangerous shoals
Lured in by
Siren song of
Sound advice
Heard it all
How better to obey
Cosa Nostra
Task at hand
Writing verse
Total gonzo
Better or worse
Read poets
Better than myself
The dead ones
Who really count
Writhing against ropes
Driven mad by mentors
Do this or that
Better if you
This was a good one
That was not
Then why, why and why

Basta I cry
Not like you
Hard enough in
My own skin
Leathered with age
Finally cut down
Friends at their oars
Never heard
Deafening silence
Gliding past sirens
Head music
Driving me mad
Taunting muse
Of self we hear
Playing my song
Not dancing to
Your tune

Stoop to Conquer

Putting kettle on
Morning coffee
Paper in the driveway
In orange plastic
Not that it matters
When it rains
Soggy news
Berkshire Eagle
Pretty vacant
Mid-December
Mild and unseasonal
Not like last year
The Horror
As Kurtz said
Dreaming of a
Green Christmas
Ain't snowing yet
I say to the locals
Blue-collar vernacular
Guys in the garage
Making conversation
Just changing tires
Cost five hundred bucks
A few things need fixing
Like me bending over
Harder every day
Picking up paper
Getting down creaky
Like chores
Once so simple
Putting on socks

Negotiating steps
In the dark
At the movies
Tuesday nights
Just five bucks
For second rate 007
Sucky Hunger Games
Life measured
In daily increments
Gradually letting go
Of bucket list
Now spelled
With an F
For the Holidays

Pill Popping

No more
Wake and Bake
Goofball
Red Sox Pitcher
Bill Lee
Spaceman
Blew World Series
Eephus pitch
Retired Tony Perez
Twice wiff-boom
Not third time
Way back, way back
Sprinkled pot on
Corn flakes
Six pills each morning
No buzz
Just staying alive
Wake and bake
Twenty-plus years ago
One month after
Meeting Astrid
Love of my life
Not so with
Jeff's 24/ 7
Reefer madness
Extolling merits
Medical marijuana
Coming soon to
Your neighborhood
Thanks pal but no thanks
Prefer a soothing

Single malt
After busy day
Boogie nights
Grooving on
Grateful Dead
Remembrance of
Things past
Better to have
Dope without hope
Than hope without dope
Cooking the rent
Up in smoke

Tom Cruise for President

Monday Chinese
Sushi House
Artists and poets
Conversation turned
To Republican pratfalls
Ship of fools
Trump as ringmaster
Hogging media spotlight
Hey Donald
You of the jingoistic
Xenophobic screed
Bulldog face
Scrunched in hate
Spewing invective
Comical comb over
You're fired
Then what
Who moves up
Most likely nominee
Tom Cruise someone said
We laughed
Don't you mean
Ted Cruz instead
Bad enough
Just think
Scientologist
In the White House
Haven't had this
Many laughs
Since Sarah Palin
Saw Russia
From her porch

Stuff

Every nook and cranny
Dishes never used
Depression glass
Bought years ago
Revere Flea Market
Worth more now
Who to sell to
Baby boomers
Retired all at once
Dumping treasures and trash
Can't give it away
Please take it
Mom would say
Empty nesters
From house to Florida
Then assisted living
Pills and meals
Home shopping
Kitsch with glitz
Genuine faux pearls
Call now and save
Utter madness of
Acquisition
Father forgive me
For collecting
Bargain hunting
Such a deal
A real steal
Seventh seal
For stuff

Great Spirit

Indian market
By the road
Navajo country
Chiseled features
Weathered and leathered
Noble and sardonic
Coyote prankster
Taunting tourists
Buying beads and trinkets
Made in China
Are you part Indian
He asked knowing the answer
Why yes I said playing along
Where do you come from
Up there I answered
Pointing to the clear
Bright cloudless sky
Hadn't heard that before
Curiously he asked
What tribe is that
Sicilian
He fell over laughing
We drove on
Through mirages
Spirits and ghosts
Monument Valley
Leaving a trail
Of red dust

Ancient Dwellings.

Classics

Arma virumque cano
Troiae qui primus ab oris
In media res
The epic hero
Aeneas escaped from Troy
Virgil's Latin version
Of Homer's Odyssey
It took a year
Boston Latin School
Told not to read
Dido and Aeneas
In the cave
Only Latin boys ever
Translate voluntarily
Other than
Winnie Ille Pu
Why bother
Learning a dead language
Can we speak it
I asked as a
Sixie tackling
Richie's First Steps
Amo Amas Amat
Six grueling years
Now gone
But for syntax
Invention of language
Tool kit for writing
French and German
Insane homework
Weekly tests

Flunked most
While teens
Other cool kids
Dated and played
Then Freshman Humanities
The Great Books
Read the Iliad
Three times
That first semester
No Cliff Notes
For C+ Earle
World's most boring professor
Magnificent works
Taught by utter mediocrity
Two semesters
He was OK for
Canterbury Tales
Recited in Olde English
Terrible for Dante
Made a mess of Cervantes
Sophomore year elective
Classical literature
Thalia Howe
Stunning Greek wife
The famous Irving
Among leftists
Black balled faculty
Brandeis during
McCarthy years
Perched on a desk
Smartly dressed

She enchanted us
Plunged into the Odyssey
T. E. Shaw's translation
A.K.A. Lawrence of Arabia
More lively than
Latimore's frigid Iliad
Those adventures
Still vivid
The Oresteia and Oedipus Rex
Aristotle's Poetics
Theories of tragedy
Within a single day
Poetry of Sappho
Hilarious Lysistrata
Never cut class
Mad crush on Thalia
Loved her as
Much as the Greeks
Classical paradigms
Shaping this verse
Decades on
Isn't that odd

Penelope

Helen
Wife of gruff Menelaus
Slut killer of men
Abducted by Paris
Pretty Trojan prince
Beloved by Aphrodite
Odysseus joined
The thousand ships
Greeks defending
Honor of brother of
King Agamemnon
Fair Penelope
With their son
Telemachus
Tending the hearth
While he partied
Half a world away
Wisest of the Greeks
Called Ulysses by Romans
A decade until the horse
That terrible night
Endless adventures
The Odyssey
Not in a rush
Enjoying epic adventures
His wife holding off
Suitors for assumed widow
Feasting in their palace
Women who wait
While men battle
So far away

No news of him
Twenty years on
From Greeks
Long since returned
At night undoing
The day's tapestry
Excuse for vigil
Ancient and weathered
Washed up near drowned
Punished by Poseidon
Blinded his son
Sheep-tending Cyclops
Saved by Athena
Not recognized
Scant resemblance of
Sanguine youth who
Sailed so long ago
Joined the contest
Who could string his bow
All tried and failed
How they laughed
When ragged vagrant
Took his turn
Cleaning house with
Hail of deadly arrows
Joined by Telemachus
By then a man
Reclaimed the bed
Of faithful wife
Long past child years
By the hearth

Tales of
Brave Ulysses
Celebrated
True heroine
Unwavering Penelope
Women who suffer
While men are away

Pope Francis

Last night
I hung out with
Pope Francis
The love
Surged through me
His warm smile
Easy beatific charm
It was electric
Come back to the Church
My son
Not hardly
Why my son
The nuns
They were mean
He nodded knowingly
A familiar refrain
In his presence
Something different
So close
Mano a mano
We touched noses
Laughing
What are you doing
For Christmas
After mass in St. Peters
Tokyo or perhaps Brazil
It's a secret
Don't tell
Or you'll go
To Hell
How long can

You keep this up
Global travel
Getting older
Pope for life
Will you retire
Like that other guy
Then two Popes
Perhaps three
Or four
Like in the
Middle Ages
Avignon and Orvieto
Turning to his aide
Smiling nun
Somber moment
Reflecting
We're thinking
About that
But not now
Or even soon
You must be busy
Thank you for visit
For you my son
Anytime
Parting he
Kissed me
On the mouth
That seemed so
Strange

Obama Cried

During a light snow
Showing his emo
New Hampshire primary
Back in 1972
Steps of conservative
Manchester Union Leader
Which attacked
Candidate Ed Muskie
Bleeding heart liberal
Democrat
Senator from Maine
Before a crush of
Probing media
He cried
Causing instant
Disqualification
No President should
Do that
Be strong for
The nation
Tough as nails
Facing travails
Standing up to
Russia
That's what it takes
Big mistake
Yesterday Obama
Did just that
Shed tears
Recalling
Senseless slaughters

First graders
Choked up
Pleading for
Gun control
End the killing
Every day in
Chicago
Freedom to worship
Trumped
That's a good one
By Second Amendment
Gun Lobby
Buying seats
In Congress
By the dozens
Millions of
Americans
Stocking up
Weapons and ammo
AK-47s for
Recreation and sport
Before it's too late
When a distraught
President
By vivid example
Gets a callous
Congress
To act on
Our behalf
Ridiculed and denounced
Last night on the news

By rabid Republicans
Armed to the teeth
Spewing lies and hate
Stating that Obama
Has gone too far
While citizens
Even toddlers
Are shot in
Crossfire
Schools, churches, mosques
Of futile debate
Nation on
Cruz control
Making a President
Weep but
Not weak

Gonzo With the Wind

Nubile teen
Palpable tension
Nervous Maggie
Windsor School
For Boston's
Smart rich girls
Quivering gaze
Anxious lust
Stammered
You remind me of
Rhett Butler
Curious
Read the book
Trashy classic
Since then have
Seen the movie
Several times
Smarmy profiteer
While Atlanta burned
Yes possibly
Some resemblance
So it seemed
At the time
More raging hormones
Than cold reason
Looking back
She married my
Friend Fred
Odd to think of this
Sad to say that today
Frankly my dear
I don't give a damn

Mea Culpa

Catholic Guilt
Sleep frenzy
Cold sweat
Rolling and tumbling
Heaven and hell
Cosmic karma
Bless me father
For I have sinned
It's been an eternity
Since my last confession
These are my sins
Yes my son
What evil have you done
Everything father
You name it
All of them
The horror
Like Kurtz in the cave
Gone mad up river
Of no return
Can you be more specific
My son
Not really
In my mind
Man is capable
Of anything
Given motive and opportunity
That's heavy
My son
Tell me about it
Deep down

I have committed
Every sin
How low do you go
Father
All of us really
Hearts of darkness
Well my son
Five Our Fathers
Five Hail Marys
Bless you my son
God forgives you
Thank you father
What a relief
Good grief

Making the Berkshires Great Again

Everyone loves us
In the summer
People come
From all over the world
Because we're terrific
You'll see
Trust me
We'll make the Berkshires
Great Again
Better than ever
It's going to be incredible
Take Tanglewood
We're going to erect a
Giant Wall
Around it
To keep bad guys out
Paid for by the Mexicans
Who will be deported
Unless they work
Hotels and restaurants
Which are huge
So hard to find help
No Muslims
Not in the Berkshires
Don't worry
Absolutely no Muslims
Unless they have money
Lots and lots of money
In what we call the hot season
It's going to be so hot
Incredibly hot

Just amazing
Jacob's Pillow
Another great one
Friends of ours
They love us
Dancing their hearts out
How about theatres
Folks we have great ones
They're going to be great
Incredibly great
With incredibly great
Musicals that are terrific
Museums are incredible
The Clark is huge
A monster
They're emptying the Prado
This summer
You'll see
MASS MoCA
Getting bigger and bigger
My friends believe me
The best in the world
And getting better
Tom Krens
Super smart
Williams graduate
Which is so terrific
He's a friend of ours
Fellow developer
All over the world
Building amazing museums

Right here in the Berkshires
Making art bigger and better
Drawing millions and millions
Of people for huge shows
Spending lots and lots
Of cold cash
Filling shops and restaurants
With seasonal workers
Guest permits
Who go back where
They belong when
We don't need them
But no Syrians
Absolutely no Syrians
This is just so exciting
Book now
Before it's too late
It's going to be great

Kid Talk

Have you tried
Talking to kids
Grandchildren
Nephews, nieces
How's school
Good
How's karate
Good
Oboe
Good
Visiting Disneyland
Good
Or teens
How's school
Whatever
Soccer
Cool
Your band
Awesome
What about adults
How are you
Don't ask
They'll tell you
In such detail
You'll
Miss the kids
So short
And sweet

Degenerate Art

Spring came
After the war
Flowers bloomed
In Flanders field
Truemmerblumen
Pushed up from
Rich compost
Corpses of
The brave fallen
Irony of war
Fertilizing beauty
So too with
Great artists
Eugene O'Neill
Tennessee Williams
Ernest Hemingway
To mention a few
But most obvious
Tormented lives
Processed as
Theatre and literature
Les Fleurs du mal
Born and died in a hotel
O'Neill like his actor dad
Drinking by eleven
Mining his family
Four Pulitzers
The Nobel Prize
American Masterpieces
His addicted mother
Thespian father

Merchant sailor
Bowery dives
All there in the work
Amazingly prolific
Defining theatre
For his era
Nasty drunk
Mean and abusive
Pissed in a bottle
Then drank it
Williams shaping his demons
Powerful plays
Mom and sister
Glass Menagerie
A treasure trove
Still sorted through
Pills and booze
Until there was
Nothing left
Hemingway
Another nasty drunk
Tales from Key West
Staggering genius
Mocked his gifted
Weaker friend
Jazz age
Drinking buddy
Scott wimpering
Out in Hollywood
Life and career in
Sad tatters

Zelda killed
In an asylum's fire
Such chilling demise
The devil's pact
Lives in the arts
Paying the price
Self-cannibalism
For the audience
We the readers
Mining for insights
Digging down into
Those dark tunnels
Veins of gold
In the black coal
Fuel of inspiration
Ernest ending it
Turning that incredible
Brain to spaghetti

Paella

Barcelona
Bright Sunday morning
After Picasso Museum
Exploring side streets
Charming bistro
Ordered paella
Observed
Elderly couple
Consuming their meal
In utter silence
Not a word spoken
Staring straight ahead
Eating with deliberation
No interaction
We wondered
Will that be us someday
Our now twenty-plus
Years of marriage
What drove them
To that solitude
Nothing left to say
Kids all grown
Grandchildren likely
It was so strange
Much later
Still recalled vividly
Now and then
We mention it
The occasional
Pause in busy lives
Constant dialogue
Recalling silent meal
In Spain

Spirit Boat. Photo-collages by Charles Giuliano

Spirit Boat

Hatshepsut
Upper and Lower Egypt
Fifth Pharaoh
Dynasty XVIII
New Kingdom
1507–1458 BC
Reigned for
Twenty-two years
Mostly at peace
Expanded trade
Mission to Punt
Land of fat queen
Here enthroned
Spirit boat
Barge on the Nile
Bound by papyrus
Vessel riddled
Slings and arrows
Assault of enemies
Many afflictions
Bone cancer and diabetes
Carcinogenic ointments
Terrible suffering
This greatest among
Ancient women
Prolific builder
Deir el-Bahri
Terraced temple
Exotic gardens
Now sand and dust
So many sculptures

Both male pharaohs
In all guises
As well as
Fair-faced queen
Body soft and feminine
Daunting paradox
Reviled by successors
Name and titles
Chiseled from cartouches

Royal Flush

Eight years younger
Prince Charles
Always seemed like
My little brother
Shared a name
Over the years
Frequent companion
Shade of night
Grouse hunting
Roaming highlands
We in kilts
He the regal tartan
Mine more garish
Traditional weave
Sicilian colors
The Queen's corgis
Nipping our heels
Balmoral Castle
Celebrating holidays
Single malt
Fit for a King
Served neat
Talk of art
Mutual interests
Reviewed his daubs
Watercolors
For Art News
Any subject
Fair game
Diana and Camilla
Off limits

Curtains drawn
The royal bedroom
Recalling 1953
Grand coronation
Pomp and circumstance
Glued to TV
Just turned teenager
Recorded the event
Dad's Dictaphone
Long lost
Seemed so epic
The years since
My pal now
Middle-aged
Like me a senior
Waiting his turn
For trip to Westminster
Kitsch and souvenirs
Public persona
Royal mania
Diana to Kate
Adorable heirs
Popping out
Future king
Posed in short pants
Such folderol
So different from
Charles I know
So well
Shall we say
Loose and relaxed

Day's end
Darkest hours
Winding down
Reflecting on
Toil of doing
Absolutely nothing
Such savoir faire

Royal Flush.

Stonehenge

From London
By train
Salisbury
Explored its cathedral
Double transepts
Built by Catholics
When Britain
Was Christian
Before Henry VIII
Mucked it up
Tea and scones
Bus out of town
Over a ridge
First glimpsed
Surrounded by fields
Ring of monoliths
Where Druids
Worshiped
Solstices
Marking seasons
Shaft of light
Dawn splitting
Stonehenge
Daunting
Keeper of time
When gods
Mattered
Eons before
Big Ben

Stonehenge.

Boulders

Forming a triangle
A kind of park
In Hartford
Caused outrage
For what was paid
Carl Andre
No stranger to
Controversy
Found not guilty
Defenestration
Artist wife
Ana Mendieta
Less is more
Deadpan
Minimalism
Placed boulders
To die for
Huge and strange
Sited along street
Wadsworth Athenaeum
Among nation's
Oldest museums
Hip-hop Hartford
Wannabe city
Insurance town
Sculptural
Risk assessment
Other end
Enhanced
Rocky shore
Washed up

Nature captured
Free of charge
Collaged as art
Conflating
Urban sublime
Facing the
Test of time

Boulders. Hartford, Connecticut.

Chateau Frontenac

On the cliff
Overlooking
Broad St. Lawrence River
General James Wolfe's
Bold strategy
Scaled its heights
Undefended
Attacked from the rear
Plains of Abraham
French and Indian War
General Louis-Joseph de Montcalm
Surrendered Quebec City
To dying British commander
Captured in painting
By Benjamin West
From our room
Historic Chateau Frontenac
Dominating the skyline
Massive and grand
Panorama of the river
Photographed Astrid
Collaged like a Hopper
Absorbing
Language, culture, cuisine
As close to Europe
Ersatz Paris
So it seems
Reached by car
Such rich flavors
Exciting the senses

Collage 305

Chateau Frontenac, Quebec City.

Views of the Chateau Frontenac in Quebec City by Giuliano.

Toledo

Until 1492
When Columbus
Sailed the ocean blue
Great scholars
Jews, Christians, Muslims
Lived and worked
Side by side
In ancient Toledo
City on a hill
Painted by El Greco
Passing through
Packa the guide
Squat and comical
With sweeping gesture
Now there are
No Jews
Visiting ancient
Synagogue
Like the mosque
In Granada
Today a church
Long ago
Borders sealed
With God on its side
Backed by Inquisition
Cure for nation
Keeping it pure
In Toledo's cathedral
Filled with gold
Where did it come from
Our student from Peru

Asked angrily
Evoking Conquistadors
Looting his ancestors
Not missing a beat
Packa explained
There were many
Gold mines
In Spain
Long before
Lorca and Franco
Blood of the poets
Soaked the land
Valley of the Fallen

Toledo, Spain.

Amalfi Coast

From Sorrento
Bus to Amalfi
Twist and turn
High on narrow cliffs
To Catch a Thief
Classic Hitchcock film
Safer to watch than
Spectacular landscape
Vertigo vistas
Views of crystal
Azure Mediterranean
Arrayed below
Quite dizzy
When we got off
Staggered to
End of pier
Thrust into calm sea
Looking back
Lush mountains
Looming over
Coastal city
On the Riviera
Where romance
Blossoms
Princess Grace
Elegant starlet
Philadelphia Main Line
Quit Hollywood
For tiny Monaco
Along the coast
Drove off the cliff

Daughter survived
Plunged to the sea
Like Icarus
Soaring aloft
Flights of fancy
Fame-melted wings
Too close to
Scorching sun
Apollo morphed
Into Dionysus

Sorrento overlooking a shaded lemon grove.

View of Amalfi, Italy.

Brandenburger Tor

Heart of Berlin
From a balcony
Apartment of
Horst and Bettina
Astrid's actor cousin
Brandenburger Tor
Not far to the right
Below day and night
Cirque de Soleil
Colorful tents
Evening strolls
Past unmarked
Cemented shut
Führer Bunker
Last days of Third Reich
Married Eva Braun
Double suicide
Red Army rolling in
Now Holocaust Memorial
Over grim last stand
Great city formerly
Divided by Wall
In the distance
Cranes towered
Over Alexanderplatz
Next visit booming but
Circus folded its tents
Couldn't afford the rent

Berlin above Cirque de Soleil.

Alpine Hotel

Back from Beantown
On the run
Hot sheet flophouse
Alpine Hotel
Lofty ambitions
Columbus Circle
Adjacent to
Huntington Hartford Museum
Now Museum of Art and Design
First night dark basement
Opened window
Looking at elevator shaft
Next day
Moved to better room
Eventually
Long term resident
Got the penthouse
Pound of pot
Good stuff
Under the bed
Subsidized gallery job
Didn't pay much
Bruno the boss
Brute not noted for
Generosity
Loved the view
Waking over
Central Park
Stretching out
Urban verdant
So rare in Manhattan

Like Lower East Side
Where I moved
303 East 11th Street
Alphabet City
Planting roots
After transient
Living out of suitcase
Pie in the sky
Down from high

Alps.

Hell's Angels

Bikers' dream
Night on Bald Mountain
Ghosts and goblins
Oozing evil
Swirl about
Tornadoes of torment
Ominous and stormy
Roil rockers
Spirit soars
Above
Winged one
Queen of darkness
Logo and guardian
Hell's Angels
Below
Under rough stones
Daunting precipice
Stacks of bikes
Oddly placid
Cupids
Seemingly
Sweet and innocent
No harm in sleep
Bad boys
Snooze
Sweet respite
From utter
Mayhem

Hell's Angels.

Kinky Boots

Take a walk
On the wild side
Clickety-click
Cloppety-clop
Lines of blow
Off you go
Plus sizes for
Tall tranny
Night crawlers
Stomping all over
Backs of Johns
Bruising and branding
Spike heels
Digging in
Feel the pain
Rough trade
Like film
Tangerine
Dark side of
LA combat zone
Thrills and danger
Lurk strolling
Mean streets
Where genders
Blend in
Exotic pleasures
Not just on
Broadway
Kinky Boots
For rube tourists
Or in edgy flicks

Turning tricks
Car hopping
Day in the life
Whom the gods love
Die young
But beautiful

Kinky Boots.

Talking Heads

Go for Baroque
Gossip
Idle chatter
Ancien Regime
Elegant salon
Madam de Pompadour
Best and brightest
Les Liaisons dangereuses
Affairs and diversions
Games of chance
Cards and dice
How very nice
Fortunes squandered
Before sobering dawn
Le Petit Trianon
Doomed Queen
Let them eat cake
Then talking heads
Dropped bloody
Into baskets
Shown to the mob
Roar of revolution
Unquenchable thirst
Reign of Terror
Glitz and glamour
Powdered wigs
Reduced to stumps
As always
Babylon Revisited
Human denatured
Conjured magic

Studio 54
Just like before
Mega-rich
Dancing the night
Away they say
Andy snapping
Polaroids
Dish and that
Rich and famous
Young and restless
Drugged and dazed
In a haze
Work as play
Purple Haze

Talking Heads.

Shanghai Dawn

Day of travel
Boston to Detroit
Then Tokyo
From there
Midnight in China
Cab drive from hell
Clutching wheel
Sweating profusely
Crawling along
Huffing and puffing
Trying to make the hill
Traffic zoomed by
Arrived at hotel
In the itinerary
Fancy and new
Huge marble lobby
Looked at our papers
You can't stay here
Chinese only
Pleaded exhaustion
Just one night
Dawn broke
Early light
First view of Shanghai
Spread below
From high-rise
Looking down
Disbelief
Astrid come look
McDonald's
Just like home

Not what we
Wanted to see

Shanghai Dawn.

Gardens of Suzhou

Utter chaos
Buying tickets
Shanghai station
Boarding train
Tea served en route
For Suzhou
Where I.M. Pei
Was born
Emerging
Astrid a redhead
Stunning
In bright light
Stopped males
Waiting to board
Dead in their tracks
Mobbed by kids
Selling trinkets and toys
Woman cab driver
Mad through streets
Pedestrians
Scrambling
Ours for the day
Visiting
Ancient gardens
Once 200 today 69
Northern Song
To late Qing dynasties
11th–19th century
Exquisite enchantment
Designed by scholars
Setting for

Study and meditation
Villas and pavilions
Lush vegetation
Rocks suggesting mountains
Vast landscapes compressed
Conjured with vivid
Imagination

Gardens of Suzhou.

Marilyn in Paris

Street corner Paris
In the Marais
Norma Jean
Not fade away
Clear light of day
Could that be
Marilyn
Some Like It Hot
Over the subway grating
Skirt billowing
Infectious smile
Tragic star
Loved by all
Including Kennedys
Happy Birthday
Mr. President
Sung in
Knowing purr
Bobby too
Mysterious death
Tipping point
When stars age
Fade away
Smarter than
We thought
Perhaps brilliant
In her way
For years
Former husband
Joe Dimaggio
Sent roses
To her grave

Marilyn in Paris.

Captured in Stone

Maine Coast
Rough
Jagged
Giant boulders
Along the shore
Bastions against
Battering sea
Pounding winter
Storms
In a niche
Nestled into
Craggy rocks
Slaves of
Michelangelo
Sculptures for
Failed project
Tomb of
Pope Julius II
Neoplatonism
He found them
Liberated
Chiseled
Hidden in
Exquisite
Carrara marble
Here returned
To nature
Writhing forever
Eternal captivity
Buried by
Stone

Collage

Captured in Stone.

Watson and the Shark

Sailing for London
Cusp of war
John Singleton Copley
Boston's portrait artist
Never to return
Struck acquaintance
Fellow traveler
Peg-legged
Scoundrel and spy
Brook Watson
No friend of
American Revolution
Related tale
Leg chomped off
Reduced to stump
Young lad
Swimming nude
Havana Harbor
Painted three versions
Boston, D.C., Detroit
Caused a sensation
Here reconfigured
Not distant Cuba
Morphed to
Artist's home
Boston during
Tall Ships
Square-riggers
Evoking
How blood
Soaked the sea

Desperation
High drama
Vividly depicted
Shark attack
Long before
Jaws

Watson and the Shark in Boston Harbor.

Niagara Falls

The American sublime
Seen from both sides
Every angle
Niagara Falls
Inspiration for lovers
Our first adventure
Decades ago
Surrounding them
Sad to say
Mostly honky-tonky
Fast food
Cheap motels
Tourist traps
Family excursions
Not our style
But the water
Pounding down
Miraculously
Cascading over us
In blue plastic
Sailing close
Overwhelmingly
Towering above
Maid of the Mist
Astrid in tears
Pure joy
Awed by nature
Once again
Close to the falls
The sound deafening
Faces drenched

Cave of the Winds
Bursting spray
Red-hot blood
Pumping through us
Hearts bursting
Moving on
In a big loop
Thousand Islands
Ending in
Erotic Montreal
Then middle-aged
Looking back
What irony
So very young
Compared to now
The passion we
Knew under a
Curtain of water
Still lingers
Mythic mist
Morning dew
Reminders of
Life we knew
With more to come

Astrid at Niagara Falls.

Name Brand

Cup of Joe
In Bologna
Where they come and go
Speaking of Michelangelo
Pip sent image
Our name on cappuccino
Giuliano
Il magnifico
Tough city
To visit
As a pious
Peace-loving
Kind and caring
Gluten-free vegan
Where the veal
Is to die for
Pity sacrificial calf
Barely weaned
Slaughtered so
Young for
Delicious meal

Giuliano Caffe, Bologna.

Elvis in London

Crossing the Thames
Millennium Footbridge
Spanning the river
To South Bank
Former power plant
Now enormous
Tate Modern
Along the shore
Historic bridges
Parliament
Big Ben
Brisk March
Spring break
Took a tour
Double-decker
Top too cold
Astrid bundled up
Face sticking out
Hood drawn tight
Raucous St. Patrick's
Celebration
Rowdy Irish
Awake all night
Pub below our room
In Piccadilly walking to
West End theaters
Club kids
Half naked
Cavorting about
Elvis looming large
Glamour and glitz

Freezing breeze
Bound to please
Randy Brits

Elvis in London.

Blinding Blizzard

Brutal blizzard
East Boston
Drifts waist high
Webster Street
Triple-decker
When Astrid
Moved in after Serbian
Tenants from hell
Harvard grad student
Skipped the lease
First floor to herself
A room of one's own
Dawn appointment
Cataract surgery
Hospital provided a car
Still dark before the T
Bizarre scene
Other patients derelicts
Knocking on gate
Like Macbeth
Murder in the castle
Comic relief
Blabbering on
About procedures
Slice and dice
Guy missing fingers
Accident prone
Emerging bandaged
Tea strainer
Over my eye
Seeing red

Back home before bed
Proposed standing up
Doctor told me
Not to bend down
On my luck

Backyard, Webster Street, East Boston.

Lion King

Ancient Assyrians
Mesopotamia
Where conflict
Raged for millennia
Now ISIS
Then kings
Killed for sport
Ersatz courage
Fighting tawny lions
Hunted from chariots
Slaughtered
Now innocents
Families in villages
Barrel bombed
Once mighty
Native warrior
Pride of the plains
Last of his race
Who roamed free
Spearing buffalo
Food for his tribe
Until dwindled
Near extinction
Manifest Destiny
White man's burden
With God on his side
Like Islam's
Assassins shouting
Allahu Akbar
What's so great
About all those
Corpses

Lion King.

Giverny Goes Pop

Rural Giverny
Monet's retreat
Eyes failing
Painting his
Lily pond
Vast panoramas
Evoking abstraction
Pushing impressionism
Once avant-garde
To its limits
Anchored to
The observed
Truth to nature
Last gasp
Of Ruskin
Lived beyond
Picasso and cubism
Changing everything
Still they joked
Not Monet but Money
Absurdity of success
After squalor
Struggle of youth
When Camille died
Here reconfigured
Deconstructed
If you will
That shimmering pond
Rich in color
Reflections of water
Now contained

As it were
By pop
Of public opinion
Moving forward
Into the beyond
At warp speed

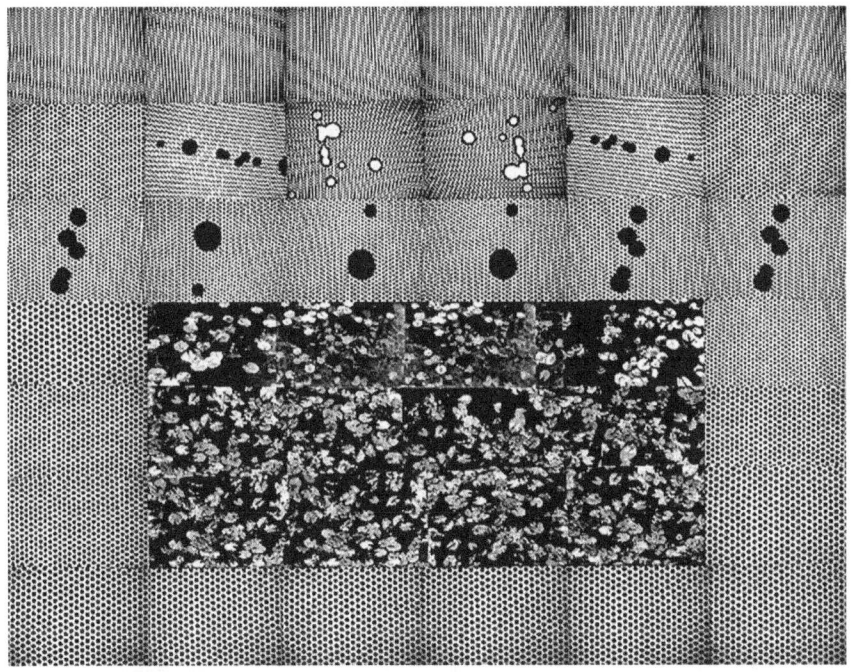

Giverny Goes Pop. Photo collage by Charles Giuliano.

Odessa Steps

Protocol
Two-plus weeks
In bed
Face down or side
No internet or TV
Keith Richards
Read by Johnny Depp
Saved my ass
The Rolling Stoned
Mick the Prick
All day NPR
News and more news
Utter bore
Enduring days
Now fifteen
Gas bubble
Slowly shrinking
Evoking Odessa Steps
Eisenstein's Potemkin
White Russians
Slaughtering rebels
Baby carriage
Caroming down
Old woman
With glasses
Shattered
Shards in eyes
Enduring ordeal
All too real

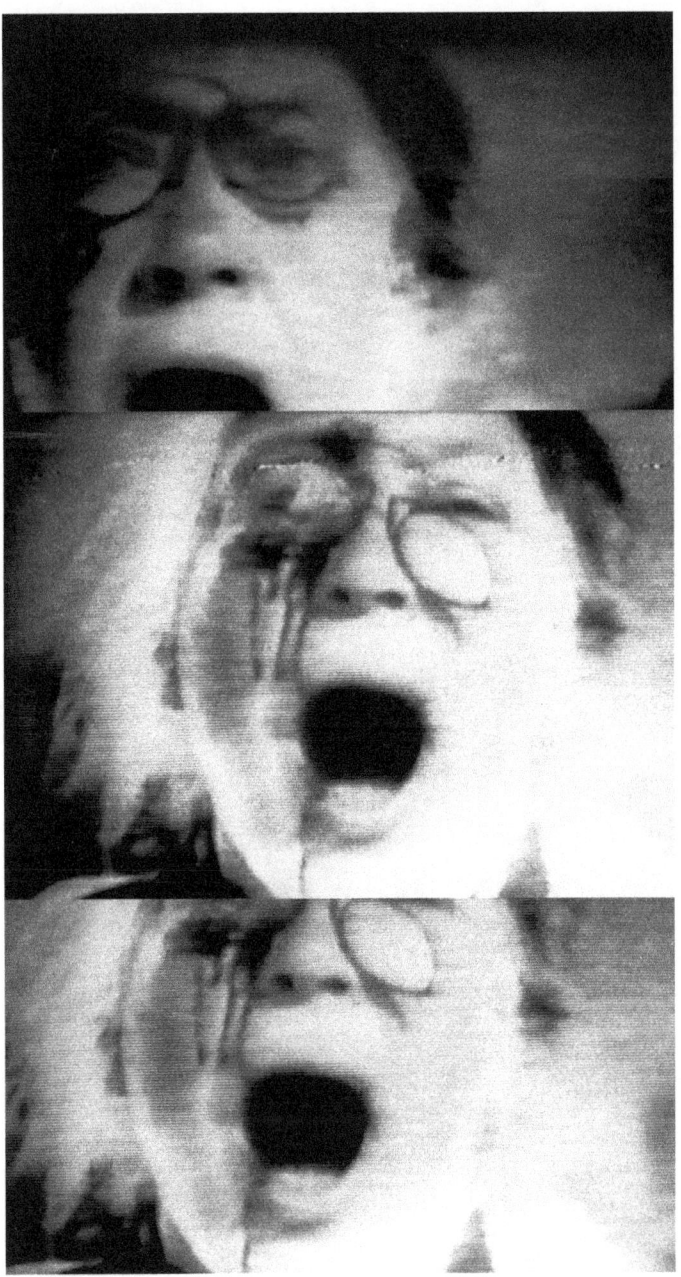

Odessa Steps.

Vacationland

Bartnick
What's in a name
Artist friend
Means
By the inn of the beekeeper
In some Eastern European
Language
For short
I called him Beekeeper
Ever droll
He never responded
To such familiarity
Or frivolity
For that matter
Contrarian
Zigged
Where others zagged
An avatar
As it were
Clipped oracles
Doled niggardly
With crisp quip
Homey twists
Ersatz Nostradamus
Beating the system
To a pulp
Frugal traveler
Hostels
Off to Italy
When school let out
After which

With Mary in Maine
Vacationland
We visited
Local haunts
On a beached dock
Next to lobster cove
Granite bridge
Inventive grid
Three of them
Frozen in time
Sitting there
Zen monks in shorts
Astrid's double vision
Thrilled to
Be by the sea

Harry, Mary, Astrid in Maine.

Caryatids

Classical Caryatid
In the British Museum
Does not belong
Stolen by Lord Elgin
Nose fell off
Punished by Athena
Violating the Erechtheum
On the Acropolis
Overlooking Athens
Porch of the Maidens
Graceful sculpture
Replaced by bare pipe
Strident insult
Brits refusing to return
Parthenon sculptures
Held hostage
Such arrogance
Looting the world
While the sun never set
Empire reduced to
Falkland Islands
Royals living on the dole
Here liberated maidens
Returned to nature
Remarkable women
Holding up the sky

Caryatids from Porch of the Maidens.

Ancient Oracles

You're not ready
Cambridge gallerist
Seymour Swetzoff said
Before my second
One-man show
In the 1960s
The first a disaster
At Hoffman/ Youngaus
On Bow Street
Above the café
Better and smarter
So I thought
Daily meditations
Basement of the MFA
Deep into secrets
Of the ancients
Read Egyptian and Tibetan
Books of the Dead
Songs of Milarepa
Consulted I Ching
Kept a diary
Of oracles
Visits to Catalan chapel
Stolen from Spain
Faith driven
Romanesque
All of that
Got into the drawing
Horror vacui
Densely packed
Sweat equity acid test

Crowded opening
Egyptians came
Dr. Smith admired
Pastel study after Rubens
Great party
North End pad
Till the brick
Smashed a window
Irate neighbors
Cops raiding
Mr. Sorentino
My landlord
Tossed them out
The kids just
Want to have fun
Seymour called
The next day
Fred C. Work
Bought that iconic
Drawing and
Several more
Mad money
Bought a used
Alpha Romeo
Temperamental
Typical Italian
Refused to
Drive in the rain
Long gone
Youthful adventure
Flashing

After images
Mandalas
Premature obsessions
With infinity
Ancient thoughts
Revisited
Still vibrant
Decades later
Clinging to
Abyss

Ancient Oracles. Drawing by Charles Giuliano.

London Calling

Spring break
Bracketing
St. Patrick's Day
Given the dissent
Odd to be Irish
Through decent
In London
Tory town
Hotel room
Over the pub
Roaring celebration
Switched rooms
Upgraded actually
To a suite
Kids setting off
Alarms all night
Evacuated
Outside until
All clear
Steps from
West End
Week of theatre
Separate seats
From the concierge
Sold out Mama Mia
Fiona Shaw
Riveting in Medea
Plays each day
Tour of city
On top of bus
Blustery and raw

Astrid bundled
Just face
Poking out
Elgin Marbles
British Museum
Lunch in the Crypt
St. Martin in the Fields
Tea overlooking
Trafalgar Square
Clogged with pigeons
Ever merry
Piccadilly Circus
Send in the Clowns
Across the pond
For a pint
Creamy hefty ale
Young's pub
Early last call
So very British
Fish and chips
With a friend
Following a crawl
Wild times
Bachelor days
Glorious youth
Just a haze
Lost in
London's fog

Astrid Bundled up in London.

Limoncello

Huge lemons
Squeezed
For limoncello
Tasty Sorrento
Pride of Amalfi Coast
Cliff-clinging buses
Terrifying ride
Positano and Amalfi
Spectacular views
Winding along
Safe on the hotel balcony
Overlooking
Shaded groves
Where they grow
Big as soft balls
Acid reflux
Taste of Italy
Aperitif
Lubricating memory
Alla tua salute

Citrus forms the basic ingredient of a refreshingly tart but sweet liqueur.

Yucca, Arizona. Giuliano photo.

Rastas in P'Town

Happy hour
Shank Painter Road
Two dozen oysters
At Mac's
Brightly colored shack
Green and yellow
Across the road
Jamaican takeout
Popped in for a look
Caribbean soul food
Ordered goat curry stew
Smiles from woman
Behind the counter
Works at our motel
Stays year-round
No time with daughter
Until late fall
Unlike Rastas
Seasonal workers
Making enough each summer
To chill in winter sun
Reggae island
Languid but poor
Taking restaurant and motel
Jobs each year
Annual migrations
Adding flavor
To fishing village
Outermost peninsula
Gone rainbow

Harvest Moon

Final twilight
Late September
Week in Truro
Like the one last May
Hop, skip and a jump
Provincetown
Tennessee Williams Festival
Ten on Tenn
Three-a-day performances
Ended this morning
Harvest Moon
Eclipse tonight
Last show
Provided by nature
As it should be
Super low tide
Hard sand
Best for walking
Breathing salt air
Face scorched
Outdoor shows
Drama and dance
The young Tenn
Vulnerable
When Kip
The dancer
Broke his heart
Forever and ever
In the village of love
Last stop before
Europe

Due East
A long swim
Even for artists and poets
Shoes full of sand
Shaken off
Back home
In the naked city

View from Gloucester motel. Giuliano photo.

Eclipse

At 9:30 last night
Stepping out from room
Motel in Truro
Onto the sand
Seat near the fire pit
Settled in looking up
It had already started
Slowly shadow inching
Over Harvest Moon
Left to right
Ever smaller sliver of light
Like a silent movie
The narration our chatter
Phenomenon of nature
First in 30 years
It was chilly
Still and strange
Astrid brought
Jacket for cool air
By the sea
A lone gull screeched
Flying by
It witnessed a miracle
Of time and space
We went inside
To watch TV
News reported
Pope flying home
Ever the skeptic
I thought of God
The vast void
And Galileo

Black Friday

Mad rush Thanksgiving
Pie then the mall
Jumping the gun
On Black Friday
Joy of giving
Buy, buy, buy
Don't let bargains
Evade your eye
Toys 'R' Us
For under the tree
Artificial ones
Last forever
Not replanted
By P'Town artist
My pal Jay Critchley
Need more irony
In marketing greed
Not the spirit
Child in the manger
Breath of livestock
Keeping infant warm
No room at the inn
Caesar's census
Under bright star
In Bethlehem
Family of David
Born to die
For our sins
At Walmart

The Reign in Spain

Tropical depression
End of September
Home from a
Glorious week
On the beach
In Provincetown
Pouring outside
Rain, rain, rain
She said
Languishing in bed
Not going to
Tai Chi this morning
Usual routine
Like Queen Elizabeth
I commented
Reign, reign, reign
While Prince Charles
Waits, waits, waits

Charleston in the rain. Giuliano photo.

Outside the Lines

I loved coloring
Turkeys for Thanksgiving
Santa Claus
During Christmas
Tacked up by nuns
Taped to windows
Gold Stars
For the best ones
Never me
Always Shelia Murphy
Neat and clean
Inside the lines
Mine scribbled and frenzied
Blur of passion
Intoxicated by
Wax on paper
Took home a stack
So proud of them
Walked up Beacon Street
To the Thorsen's
Three daughters
One my age
At Mt. Alvernia Academy
Catholic rich kids
Rare in Brookline
Rang the bell
Small vestibule
They weren't home
Waited and waited
Had to pee
Did all over

Got scared
Mopped it up
With my drawings
Stuck to the walls
To dry
Finally went home
For supper
Leaving behind
First of many
Exhibitions

An early self portrait as a tramp.

Turkeys

That first Thanksgiving
Harvest celebration
Neighbors later obliterated
Brought wild turkeys
Like the flock
In our backyard
Devastated by bird flu
Loss of millions
But not ours
Plentiful at Big Y
Even a coupon
Seven-dollar rebate
Just the two of us
Home alone
Perhaps joining friends
Years ago in New York
Far from family
Invited to Queens
Uncle Bill
His French wife
Brought out the bird
With white wine glaze
Truly amazing
A Gallic twist
For American classic
Truth is just roasted
It can be bland
Best part always
Lots of stuffing
Slathered with gravy
Remembering this year

Those slaughtered
In Paris or mean streets
Back home
Yet again
We sit in peace
Tattered brotherhood
Having our fill
Under a tarnished
White flag

A turkey drawn in 1945 with my name misspelled by a nun.

Low Winter Sun

Night comes early
Dark by four
Not just days
But hearts and minds
Dig in ever deeper
Not gloom as such
Balance from summer's
Deceptive optimism
Winter is time for
Epic poetry
Gloucester shipwrecks
In Olson's Maximus
Thick tome
Measured out like
Cornflakes
Ten pages with breakfast
Wandering through
Dogtown where
Nugents farmed
In my blood and DNA
The inner Rockport
Winter is when
We wander down
Rabbit hole of self
Turning over
Hurtful memories
Those who injured us
Not friends
Or even truly enemies
They annoyed our youth
Were rivals of

Sanguine ambitions
Progress sorted out
Over time and distance
Fate and scores settled
Stories of their afflictions
Accounts of tragedy
Travails of others
Like Olson's fishermen
Foundering in the depth
Of cold unforgiving
Oceans those
Titanic storms at sea
Waves crashing over
As well as within
Epic winter of
Our discontent
Made more glorious
The return of Persephone
From Hades
To Mother Earth
Flora tossing flowers on
Caves and graves
Where now
During arctic December
There is scant
Light

Santa

North Pole
Wicked cold
A few days before
Christmas
Knocked on the door
Ancient weathered wood
An elf answered
What do you want
Have to speak to Santa
How did you get here
JetBlue to Alaska
Walked from there
Terrible flight lousy snacks
Our location is secret
A myth you know
How did you find us
Googled then GPS
Kids in the Berkshires
Where I come from
Are worried
Not a flake of snow
What about the sled
The reindeer are getting old
Santa's getting up there too
Will he make it this year
Just need a few minutes
Then I'll go
Well if you insist
Come sit by the fire
We put in a gas log
A few years back

Better than splitting wood
Too busy making toys
Much more complex
We sent an elf to MIT
Subcontracts and all that
IPhones and tech stuff
Not like it used to be
Yo Ho Ho
Jolly fellow entered
Full white beard
Long johns and slippers
Enormous belly
Sat beside me
Next to ersatz hearth
People say we look alike
I stammered
Somewhat awed
How are you holding up
You must be in the hundreds
Old and overweight
I sat on your knee
Years ago at Filene's
You brought me a sled
Flexible Flyer
Lots of snow back then
Great sigh
It gets tougher every year
Especially for kids
Immigrants and refugees
Such turmoil and hate
Hard to spread my love

The elves have been great
We work with computers
Keep up with wish lists
By e-mail starting
Back in July
After vacation
Viking River Cruise
Mrs. Claus and I
Loved the buffet
Tell the kids back home
Cookies and milk
Look up in the sky
You'll see us
Fly by
Thanks for coming
Merry Christmas

Me and Santa.

Winter's Tale

The night is cold
Late December
Nearly Christmas
Come friend
Sit with me
Close to the hearth
Watch the flames
Ever brightly changing
Hot sparks dancing
Lean closer
Something I must say
Whispered
By the fire
For your ear only
To hear
Secrets told to me
Long years
Pondering them
Odd and lonely
Passed on
Now to you
Tell no one
Promise me
Until it's time
There dear one
Now you know
As did our
Ancestors
Struggled
Through their hours
As do we

Take my hand
This is the poet's
Well-guarded grip
In our genes
Shared memory
Come that day
When all will
Be revealed
With such dismay
To those trusted
Few and brave
Beneath the tree
That shades in summer
Warmth
Like now
Come winter
While we wait
Drowsy and sedate
For return of
Persephone
From dark Hades
Her living hell
Joining ours on earth
With no exit

Shaker Village in Winter. Giuliano photo.

Day After Christmas

Santa is pooped
Sleeping it off
Back at the Pole
Tended by Mrs. Claus
Hot chocolate
Warm thick blanket
Same scenario
UPS and the Post Office
Delivering all those
Last minute gifts
Extra pounds from
Festive parties
Cookies and fruitcake
Hearty eggnog
With a blast of rum
Celebrations with
Friends and family
Renewing traditions
Leftovers tonight
Then turkey soup
Peace on earth
Universal truce
Slipping away
Inevitable return
Hate and killing
Good will
Packed away till
Next year
Yet again
Dark cloud
Prince of Darkness

Casts its shadow
Long dead of winter
Sorry kids
Enjoy the toys
But Christmas
Was yesterday

33rd Annual Re-Rooters Day Ceremony

Families spend
Megabucks
Lighting the tree
Brightening homes
During holidays
Joy for children
Then unceremoniously
Stripped of decorations
Dry needles shedding
Heaved in trash
Seduced and abandoned
Undignified detritus
Waste and disgrace
Provincetown artist
Jay Critchley
Honors these
Wounded warriors
Signifiers of forests
Feng shui
Nature and environment
Re-rooters Day
Now 33rd year
Tree Valhalla
Given Viking burial
Burned in a boat
Floating out to sea
Honored with ceremony
Wishes and resolutions
Offerings to flames
Chanting along the shore
Spirit of Christmas

Laid to rest
Respect and pageantry
After Twelve Days
Of stockpiling
Yet again January 7
Dead of winter
Long dark nights
While Druids
Dream

Jay Critchley in his Provincetown yard with Christmas Trees. Giuliano photo.

Valentine

Dead of winter
Hunkered down
Record cold
Windchill 25 below
Instant frostbite
Mid-February
Wicked weather
In the Berkshires
Annual beard
Since the Holidays
Mountain Man
A guy thing
Shaggy-faced
Like Santa Claus
She said with an edge
Valentine's Day
Cleaned the face
Neat and trim
With love
Best I can give
Being as how
We live
Nowadays
You look younger
Smiling and pleased
With words
Going to my head
Astrid steady on
Always there for me
Thick and thin
Hanging in

Some early
Spring-cleaning
Wool sheared
Not just sheep
While flowers
Sleep

Astrid on the beach in Florida. Giuliano photo.

Who

Who are you
Seemingly familiar
Then not
Spectral face haunting
Hints of apricot
Aspect of minerals
Perhaps volcanic
Savoring taste
Flavors of past
Note in a bottle
Once Cabernet
With sorbet
Cast adrift
Desperate clue
Sent by you
Marooned
Tropical and topical
Archipelago
Tiny island of memory
Evoking presence
I have you not
Come near
That I might
Grab your throat
Choking out truth
Elusive oracle
Solving the riddle
Now mocking me
Your Cheshire grin
How grim
This reaper
Of abandoned souls

Who You

Who
May I speak with
Regarding what
She asked
Utter mayhem
Nightly news
Global disasters
Home and abroad
Collateral damage
Acts of God
Can I talk to Him
Finger-pointing
Blame game
Millions of refugees
Boat people
Corpses in the sea
Cruz calls for
Carpet-bombing
Securing borders
Muslims and Mexicans
Scorched earth
Drought and famine
Children eating dirt
Drug cartels
Corporations
One-percenters
Snouts in the trough
Put me through
To the Boss
He's busy sir
With other matters

Thanks for your patience
Not to worry
It's an election year
Things will be better
Can I put you on hold
Till we have a
New President
Thanks for your concern
Have a nice day

When

When
Does this make sense
Finally something
Meaningful
That hasn't been
Written
Too many times
Musty verse
Nothing new
Under this sun
Fuckit lists
How to avoid
Platitudes
Glory of nature
Sunsets
Surfing in Paradise
Exotic adventures
Friends who find
Visiting Cuba or India
Disappointing
The inconveniences
Compared with
Getting a NY cab
In the rain
So much for the
Taj Mahal
Precious nuggets
Information and insights
Connecting the dots
Necklace of pearls
Strung out striving

Beyond the ordinary
Genuine faux
Endless lies
Sorted through
Lives frontloaded
For my generation
Drugs, sex, rock 'n' roll
Now penance and pills
Measured in doses
Existential methadone
Not getting buzzed
Diet and exercise
Hanging on tight
Seatbelts fastened
What became of
All that raging
Sweaty sex
Like you see on TV
Millennials
Hooking up
Sanguine potential
Deferred to now
Last shootout
OK Corral
Hipster gunslingers
Rock stars
Dropping like flies
Reminder that
All is vanity
Losing grip
On our sanity

Why

Why me
They ask
Familiar conundrums
With no answers
Afflicted
Pain and suffering
Human condition
Burden of life
Castle to hovel
Where was God
In the death camps
No poetry after Auschwitz
Lament of Chosen people
Or Syria
Assad bombing
His own people
Scattered blown asunder
While ISIS
Beheads infidels
Where is He
Bedsides of diseased
Riddled with cancer
Children of famine
Thin as sticks
Too faint for lessons
Why me they ask
The Creator
Lends a deaf ear
Job's wife said
Curse God and die

Where

Where am I
Jolting awake
Disembodied
Edge of forever
Flatland
Hic transit dracones
Like medieval maps
Jerusalem
Where Jesus preached
Christocentric
Epicenter of the universe
Fact trumped by
Catechism
God made me
As politicians
Bless themselves
To get votes
In the Heartland
Eyeless in Gaza
Epiphany
Thrown from a horse
Road to Damascus
Blind faith
World saviors
Jihadists
Blown to bits
Floating by
Not making sense
In outer limits
Lacking landmarks
Road rage

Blizzard white-out
Post Newtonian
Time warp
Stupor of mundane
Where all is OK
Midnight at the oasis
While camels sleep

Where From Here

Where do we come from
D'ou venons nous
As Gauguin asked
In that epic work
Intended as his last
Diseased in Tahiti
Paradise as hell
Botched suicide
Reaching back
My DNA
Millions of years
From caves to condos
Ends with me
No issue
Last of Mohicans
It would seem
The gift of life
So precious
But hardly rare
Our fragile planet
Coping with billions
Exhausting resources
Ravaging Mother Earth
Numbers ever growing
Economies in turmoil
Arguably a contribution
Not to reproduce
Moving forward
Future millennia
Genes passed on
Words and deeds
Such as these

Never Neverland

What happened
An incident
Not unusual
Everyone eventually
Where am I
Nowhere
Or everywhere
Now what
Nothing
Forever
That's a long time
Can I see Mum
Of course
Where is she
In your heart
As always
Heaven or hell
Does it matter
Not really
Just curious
Feeling anxious
Can I take something
Speak to somebody
That depends
Nothing really
Matters
Anymore
Another fine mess
Did you think
It would be different
Not really

Where are the
Saints and martyrs
Busy
Guess I'm not one
So it seems
Hope you're not
Disappointed
Perhaps a bit
Just relax
It's all OK
Day by day
From here
To Eternity

Space Oddity

Way out there
Eons ago
Billions of miles
When black holes
Smashed together
Swallowing
Dual voids
Cosmic event
Good vibrations
Warping
Time and space
As Einstein predicted
Now proven
Eureka moment
How insignificant
We are
Grain of sand
On universal beach
Gazing up
At the twinkling
Unknown
So taken
With our
Puny significance
In vast beyond

Shooting Into the Ranks

More funerals than weddings
The hourglass flipped
More sand on bottom than top
Shocked by death of Paul
Artist and colleague
By motorcycle last week
At barely 49
Doing the math of survival
Struggling to outlive assets
Ever diminished resources
Lunch with colleague
Discussing symptoms
Sharing those of friends
At theatre last night
Hearing of a conflict
Three funerals in one day
Opted to stay home
Rather than insult them
With his absence
Impossible to decide
They come in clumps now
Like twenty-somethings
Starting families
Focus on elaborate celebrations
Outspending each other
Burials are more modest
Solemn and sincere
Not being around to hear
What's said of us
Asked what he would say
Given the occasion

Paused to consider
Put on the spot
Insightful and oblivious
Blurted out with laughter
Over won ton

Requiem

Neverland
Forever
Over there
Five long days
From here
All hope
Abandoned
Ties severed
Now wild man
Final trek
Sunup to sundown
First light to darkest night
Trudging on
Blazing desert
Parched mouth
Burning feet
Endurance complete
Staggering on
To the forest
Through the trees
Ripped by thorns
Up over mountains
Numbing cold
Drifts of snow
Bleak and beautiful
Crossing freezing rivers
Drenched and drowned
Shivering alone
Up at dawn
Hardly rested
Moving on

To the shore
Crafting a raft
From driftwood
Toward island
Of no return
For which
By then
So many ordeals
He yearned
For closure
Finally
Over

Checkmate

On a cliff
High above the sea
Waves crashing below
The Knight opened
Advancing a pawn
After intensive study
Death countered
Classic strategies
Played for life itself
Each day at dusk
They met in combat
Game of wits
Highest stakes
They opened a rare bottle
Well-aged vintage
Carefully decanted
On day one
Elegant, creamy, glycerol
Hidden minerality
Swirled in tall glasses
Exploding aromas
Returned to the board
The Knight attacked
The tannins had settled
Lush ripe cherry flavors
The sunset ending play
Resumed next day
Becoming more intense
Lavender prevailed
Followed by smoked chorizo
Death in retreat

Day four approached endgame
Aromas of strawberries and hazelnuts
Ended in a draw
Death vanished at dawn
Inevitably to return

Lazarus

Fine sendoff
Fragrant flowers
Ancient rituals
Burnt offerings
Copious libations
Eloquent eulogies
Sobbing loved ones
Widow bent low
Inconsolable
Mary took pity
He entered crypt
Pulled back shroud
Lazarus emerged
Blinded by
Light of day
That rarest journey
Dark land crossed over
From which
No traveler returns
Wild jubilation
They danced for joy
Feast and celebration
Back home at dawn
Time passed
Symptoms returned
Filled with melancholy
Too weak to work
Called back
From eternal rest
Wasted away
Yet again

Sallow flesh
Sinking deeper
Cursed her
Seeming good deed
Miracle
A second time
Soon dead
Modest burial
Few attended
No tears shed
Just eternity
Instead

Copyright

Front cover "Spirit Boat" photo collage, copyright Charles Giuliano, 2016.

Back cover author photo by Astrid Hiemer, copyright, 2016.

Essay and poems by Charles Giuliano, copyright by Charles Giuliano, 2016.

Essay by Robert Henriquez, copyright by Robert Henriquez, 2016.

Vintage images, Family, pages 1 to 27, copyright Giuliano family archive, 2016.

Photo of Steve Nelson, page 39, courtesy of and copyright by, Steve Nelson, 2016.
Photo of the Modern Lovers, page 206, copyright Steve Nelson, 2016.

All photos, photo collages, and drawings, copyright Charles Giuliano, 2016.

www.ingramcontent.com/pod-product-compliance
Lightning Source LLC
Chambersburg PA
CBHW031130160426
43193CB00008B/87